WHITES CROSSING

By
Donald J. Rowland

Sunset Publications
Carlisle, PA

*This book is affectionately dedicated
to my family, all the old friends
who inspired the stories told here,
and to the way things were in the days
of our youth at Whites Crossing.*

Published by
Sunset Publications
205 Acre Drive
Carlisle, PA 17013

Copyright © 1995 by Donald James Rowland

All rights reserved. No part of this book may be reproduced or transmitted in any form or by any means, electronic or mechanical, including photocopying, recording, or by any information storage or retrieval system, without the written permission of the Publisher, except where permitted by law.

Library of Congress Catalog Card Number: 96–92135
    Rowland, Donald J.
    Whites Crossing
ISBN 0–9653407–0–8
Manufactured in the United States of America

October 1996

Acknowledgment

There are many who helped to make this book a reality, and I would be remiss if I did not acknowledge that fact.

My brother, Pat Rowland, and sister, Ruth Rowland Markunas, provided extensive details on our family history, some of which I had forgotten. As the work progressed, they remained partners in its development by reading every chapter and offering critical comment. Their assistance was inestimable and I am gratefully indebted to them.

Nellie Oblazney provided extensive, colorful details about my maternal grandparents and the place of their birth. Nearing one hundred years of living, her keen memory made her an extraordinary oral historian on Poland and Whites Crossing. Her son, Frankie, supplied additional insights and served as a very able interpreter between his mother and me. Jenny Williams was also a constant reference source whose knowledge of the Whites Crossing area helped to enrich the story. Each of them has my sincere gratitude.

I am particularly grateful to Hank Loftus, Jr. for the information he researched and shared on the background of the Rowland family. His contributions and the insights graciously given by my father's youngest sister, Kitty Rowland Noone, were invaluable.

A sincere thank you to Ruth McDonald Neary, teacher and former neighbor, for her first-hand account on how things were at the old schools in Whites Crossing.

And a very special appreciation goes to my wife, Lillian, for her exceptional patience and support during the many months this story was researched and written.

Contents

	Prologue	vii
1	The Village	1
2	A Bungalow Home	7
3	Bialka	13
4	Passage to America	17
5	The Meeting	23
6	The Irish Factor	27
7	Pat and Mary	33
8	View From a Front Porch	41
9	Babkee and Jadkee	59
10	A Winter of Dark Mornings	79
11	Red Racer Wagon	91
12	Blue Shirts and Gray Knickers	99
13	Lady of the House	107
14	Post Cards From the Past	117
15	While Waiting for a War	147
16	The Home Front	159
17	Visit From a War Plane	167
18	Last One in Line	179
19	Coming Home	187
20	The *Mary K* and Crew	197
21	A Long Ride South	203
22	An Unexpected Silence	211
	Epilogue	225
	Afterword	227

Prologue

There is in the lives of most people a Whites Crossing. More than a place, it represents a time of life when all experiences are new and each serves to add to the character of the person we eventually become. From the vantage point of maturity, it is possible to examine the days of our youth in a meticulous but objective fashion, taking pleasure from the multitude of pleasant memories but not being too concerned about some of the harsher realities of life. Adversities big and small are as much a part of the living and learning process as the happenings that are more warmly recalled. All experiences, good or bad, leave a lasting impression, and we are not at liberty to selectively choose only those we like. Each contributes to the individuals we become as we pass from youth into adulthood because, one theory holds, "you are what you were when..." when we were young, developing, and being molded by family, friends, and the community in which we lived.

CHAPTER 1

The Village

◆◆◆

*W*hites Crossing lies tucked away in the extreme northeast corner of Pennsylvania, right at the edge of the anthracite coal region, about sixteen miles from Scranton. There are a number of ways to get to Whites Crossing from Scranton, but the more scenic route, the one that gives the richer flavor of the area and its people, is to pass through the small towns that are strung out along the Lackawanna Valley like outposts on a long meandering trail through a prime section of that old anthracite field. The variety of names, such as Dickson City, Olyphant, Peckville, Mayfield, and Carbondale, does not disguise the fact that there is a comfortable sameness to all the towns and the people who live in them. They are, for the most part, descendants of immigrants, people whose ancestors came from various parts of Europe starting in the mid-1800s and continuing through the early 1900s. Their common goal in coming to the area was to improve their lot in life. There are those who would dispute the fact that they could do so in the coal mines of northeastern Pennsylvania, but there is no debate about the effort they made to establish roots in a foreign country for the generations that would follow them. They were hard-working, friendly, supportive, deeply religious and fiercely determined to be successful. Each town had its ethnic churches, many with a social hall nearby, and all had general stores and taverns, many taverns.

The main road out of Carbondale, Route 6, follows Canaan Street uphill for just over a mile. At a point where the road makes a sweeping right turn to take traffic over the Moosic Mountains, a road to the left, lined with trees for a short distance, leads to Whites Crossing. At the center of the small village the road branches in two directions; the left branch slopes downhill to the community of Simpson while the right branch is a sharp incline toward the nearby mountains.

At one time a railroad passed through the center of Whites Crossing, but by 1936 only the abandoned railroad bed remained. The land on which the village stands, and much of the surrounding area, belonged to the White family. This linking of the White family name with the railroad crossing probably began as a way to identify the location and over the years became the formal name for the village.

In 1936 the village of Whites Crossing had approximately fifty homes scattered over six streets or roads. The longest, Number Four Road, is an uphill route to the reservoir that inspired its name, Number Four Pond. At most, about two hundred people lived in or near the village. Most of the men worked in nearby coal mines or in jobs related to the coal industry. Few women worked outside the home, and those who did most likely worked in the textile mills located in Simpson. Many of the families engaged in farming on a small scale, mostly to meet the needs of the family. They raised a few cows for milk and beef, had chickens and ducks, perhaps a hog, and every family had a vegetable garden during the growing season.

The people who settled in Whites Crossing were mostly Polish, Slovak and Russian, with a sprinkling of Irish and Italians scattered throughout the area. Each group brought from their native land customs, rituals, and ethnic foods, things that were essential parts of their lives in another time and place. The variety of people, traditions, languages and foods added a certain color, richness and spice to the community, a blending of old cultures in a new environment. Maintaining old traditions from the motherland, however, extended even to the churches they founded and attended. While most of the people were Catholic, each ethnic group insisted on having their own ethnic church. As a result, within a distance of a mile and a half at most, four Catholic churches could be found. Although most churches bore the name of a specific saint, most people referred to them as the Polish Church, Slovak Church, Irish Church and Italian Church. Since Latin was then the standard language for the mass at all Catholic churches, the major advantages of belonging to an ethnic church included hearing sermons in your native tongue and having a priest who understood your culture and background. Maintaining ethnic churches, cultural traditions and rituals served to keep each group intact and, at the same time, helped people retain an emotional connection with their place of birth, a place few would likely see again.

At the center of the village, where the road branched and the old railroad crossing remained as evidence of more prosperous times, were three taverns. All stood within a few hundred feet of each other. At one time there was a fourth tavern in the same central area of the village, but it did not have the longevity of the other three. None of the taverns had fancy names; each bore the name of the owner. In 1936 the three taverns in Whites Crossing were Billy Kresock's, John Costolnick's and Louie Novobilski's. It was the custom of most miners in those days to stop at one of the taverns on their way home from work to wash the coal dust from their throats with a whiskey and beer. The standard order for the bartender was to provide a "shot and a beer." The drink, taken in the company of fellow miners and local friends, provided a period of relaxation after long hours of manual labor in an underground coal mine. More than just a stopping place on the way home from work, the taverns were also places where husbands and wives met with friends to eat, drink, exchange information on a variety of family matters and just plain gossip. They were social centers, places where one could take a break from the rigors of both work and life.

Along with the taverns, Whites Crossing had three grocery stores. Like the taverns, each bore the name of the family that owned the store. The largest, Fedor's, was near the center of the village and was more of a general store than the other two. It had a large selection of groceries, a butcher shop, a clothing and general dry goods section, plus hardware. Just inside the entrance to the store, a glass counter contained a variety of penny candy. The children of Whites Crossing had a keen interest in that particular display. A concrete pad, six feet in depth and as wide as the storefront, provided space for parking wagons and sleds. At the edge of the concrete pad, next to a paved road, was a single Texaco gas pump.

Fedor's was a busy store, where customers waited in line at the butcher counter for service. It was a place where people were sure to see many of Whites Crossing's residents, which made going to Fedor's both a social and shopping event. It was a major part of the community because of the large variety of items available, and for those families encountering special financial hardships during the Great Depression, buying on credit was always an option. The liberal credit arrangements instituted by the founders of the store, Frank and Nellie Fedor, made it possible for many families to survive during periods when incomes were small or nonexistent.

Rushen's store was about a hundred yards up Number Four Road from the railroad crossing. It was smaller than Fedor's and specialized only in groceries. However, many children walking to the elementary school passed by Rushen's store. Since it was the last opportunity to buy penny candy on the way to classes, many young customers made a brief stop to buy some sweets before continuing on to school. The third store, operated by the Pilny family, was on the road to Simpson. This store had six steps leading to a covered entrance, much like a porch, because the basement for the building was above ground. Quite small, it seemed more aligned with the community of Simpson. It was a place we did not visit very often since Fedor's store was larger and more convenient for us to reach.

The elementary school for Whites Crossing children was halfway up steep and winding Number Four Road. At one time there were two schools at this location. The smaller building had classes for the first three grades while the larger school building held classes for students in grades four through eight. One day in February 1937, during a blizzard, the smaller school caught fire over the lunch hour and burned to the ground. Since all the children walked home for lunch, no students were there when the fire started. However, we did rush back with more than a little glee to watch this spectacular blaze. Our excitement over the prospects of being excused from going to school for the balance of the year was short-lived; within a few days we were sharing crowded class space with other grades in the remaining building.

While occasionally there were more than two grades in a room, two was the norm and both grades shared the same teacher. The remaining school, named Robert Morris, had four classrooms with wooden desks anchored to oiled wooden floors, indoor bathrooms and a long hallway where the single pencil sharpener for the school hung on the wall. Open space surrounded most of the school and provided a lot of room to run and play during recess. A patch of nearby woods attracted the more adventuresome students to follow the well-worn paths through the hilly wooded area. A ball field at the rear of the building was also used extensively. Each of the twice-daily recess periods ended with a signal from the principal ringing a hand-held bell. Students would line up according to grade and the upper grades had the privilege of going in last. The mode of transportation to and from school was walking, including the trip home for lunch, and bad weather was not a reason for cancelling classes.

CHAPTER 2

A Bungalow Home
♦♦♦

Our home was not actually within the village of Whites Crossing. We lived on the upper end of Canaan Street, just a short distance from where the road to Whites Crossing branched left off Route 6. We were outside the city limits of Carbondale and not quite in Whites Crossing, at least not physically. But our affinity was clearly with Whites Crossing for there were our people. Here was where we went to school, played, shopped for groceries, raced our sleds down Number Four Road and skated on a place called the "greenie pond." This was the place where most of the elders, including my maternal grandparents, spoke in a language we did not understand very well. Their children, born in America, could speak the native language of their parents and English as well. However, most of the grandchildren, myself included, had become too Americanized to understand the speech of our grandparents. At best, we knew some basic words of the their language and developed a sense for what they were telling us. They, in turn, used a combination of their native tongue and some English words to converse. More often than not, we understood each other. It was a unique way of communicating; it seemed to fit perfectly with all the other things we had in common, and in some special way, it added to the bonds we had with each other and the community.

The land on which our home stood was part of a small farm my grandparents bought about 1904. Their purchase included the farm land, a house and a barn. Later, they would build another house next to the one they originally acquired and make it the family homestead. Our lot, deeded to my parents for $1.00 in 1924, bordered Route 6. Other lots taken from the farm also faced this main road. Eventually, six houses lined our side of the street, four occupied by relatives and two by good neighbors. At the far left of the farm was a house occupied by my grandparents' son, Joseph. My grandparents lived in the next house, my Aunt Annie lived in the third, ours was fourth, the Zukowski family lived next to us, and the Falong family had the last house on that side. On the opposite side of the road, directly across from my Aunt Annie's location, stood an elegant house occupied by the McDonald family. They also owned a huge hay field, about sixteen acres, which separated their house from that of their neighbor on that side of the road, the Calafut family. The eight houses made up our "block," a small, close-knit neighborhood. One of the great pleasures of living so near to close relatives and good friends was the feeling of being at home, no matter whose house you happened to be in at the time.

The house my parents built, called a bungalow, had a basement wall that was partially above ground. As a result, it had a raised appearance and at the front entrance seven steps led to a porch that extended along the entire front of the house. It was a simple, one-story structure with a small dormer on the roof above the porch to allow light into the attic. The wood siding was white and the floor of the porch was gray. The porch had a railing along the front and sides, a natural support for those who liked to sit with their feet propped up. Along the base of the porch was latticed woodwork enclosing the space beneath the porch. On the right side, part of the lattice was made into a hinged doorway to allow access to the space. While used for storage of certain items, to me it was much more valuable as a kind of secret place to play, store treasured toys and be alone.

The front door was in the center of the porch and opened into the living room, or parlor, the more common term for that room. Immediately to the right of the front door entrance was my parents' bedroom. A wide opening led from the parlor into a sitting room that was similar in size. To the right of this room was the second bedroom. At the back wall of the sitting room, on the left, was an entrance to a large pantry. Along with the storage of canned goods, pots, pans and dishes on shelves that lined the right wall of the pantry, a tall chest of drawers contained towels of all types, table cloths and some clothing. Next to the pantry, also accessed from the sitting room, was a small walk-in closet, the only closet in the house. A doorway not far from the closet led to the kitchen, which was located immediately behind the second bedroom.

The kitchen was not large, but it was a very cozy place, especially during the winter months. The coal-burning stove, complete with oven and a food warming storage bin above the cooking surface, had a place of prominence in the kitchen. A round table and an assortment of chairs completed the furnishings. In the right hand corner was a small sink with a single faucet that supplied only cold water. In the left corner of the kitchen, right behind the walk-in closet, was an access to the basement. Normally, the access remained covered by a hinged floor that we called a "trap door." At one time or another each of the children in our family tumbled down the basement stairs when the trap door was open. It seemed to be a family tradition. When the trap door was in the down position, the space served as a small pantry. Shelves along the far end of this narrow, hall-like area provided storage space for groceries. From the kitchen a back door opened onto a small porch which provided access to the backyard and to a driveway that ran along the right side of the house to a single car garage. The garage housed the family car, a two-door 1931 Chevrolet Victoria Coupe. Painted black, with red wire wheels, it was my father's prized possession.

The basement had a ceiling that was barely six feet from the floor. A large coal bin occupied the corner beneath the kitchen, and shelving, which lined most of the walls, stored a variety of items, including fruit, jam, vegetables, jelly, catsup and relishes canned by my mother. In the center of the basement was a coal-fired, hot air furnace. Above the furnace, cut into the floor between the parlor and sitting room, was a large metal grate. The grate allowed the hot air from the furnace to rise to the first floor and heat the house. Heat pipes did not extend to individual rooms. This furnace was a gift to my parents from our neighbors, the McDonald family, when they had it removed from their home and replaced by a new heating system. In our home the hot air furnace replaced the original heating plant, a pot-bellied stove that occupied a space along the wall between the second bedroom and the entrance to the kitchen. The simple hot air furnace was a big improvement in heating the house, but it was not as colorful as the old pot-bellied stove.

At the rear of the basement was a door that allowed access to the outside through six stairs and dual trap doors that sheltered the entrance from the elements. Since it was usually cool in this area, it often served as a place to store cooked food and desserts. The walls of the basement received a coat of whitewash each year; it was something we did in the spring. Keeping it in good order was important because we used it as a part of our living area. We stored food, clothing, tools and playthings in the basement. It also served as a laundry room, complete with lines for drying clothes when weather did not permit outside drying. The basement was a great place to play games with friends when the weather was stormy or too hot to be outside.

Our home had no bathroom facilities; the single cold water faucet in the kitchen and another in the basement were the only indoor plumbing. The main pantry served as a place for taking baths. We used a large, round galvanized tin tub and water heated on the kitchen stove. Following a bath, carrying the tin tub outside to be emptied was awkward. An outhouse, located on a small rise about one hundred feet from the back of the house, was our toilet. Getting there during a downpour or blizzard could be a challenge. Making a night visit under such conditions could be a real test of character. We never felt deprived, however, because we did not have the more comfortable accommodations provided by indoor bathroom facilities. That is the way it was for just about every family in the area. Almost every backyard had an outhouse at the far end of the property; and most had a portable bathing tub of some sort. It was the standard of the time and was simply accepted as a part of life.

On January 1, 1936, there were seven people living at our home: my parents, Patrick and Mary, their four children, and Mary Lesneski, an "adopted" child. The oldest of the children was Pat, about six months shy of thirteen. Ruth was almost ten, I was about eight and a half and Gene had just been born, the first baby of the New Year in the Carbondale area. There would have been a fifth child in the family at that time but my mother's firstborn, Marian, died of diabetes in 1924.

Mary Lesneski came into our family about 1927. At the time my mother had three small children and was trying to maintain a job in a textile mill located in Simpson. Although my father had a full-time job, the second income was necessary to help with the mortgage and the expense of supporting a growing family. As they looked for someone to help with household chores and care for the children while they worked, my parents learned of a ten-year-old girl who desperately needed a home. The Lesneski family lived in a cabin located in a heavily wooded area just north of

Simpson, a place called Old Slope. The family was living in extreme poverty and Mrs. Lesneski, seriously ill, could no longer care for her children. Although no formal adoption took place, it helped both families when Mary came to live with us. Mary would stay with us for about twelve years, until she got married. In all respects she was a member of our family, an older and wiser sister who shared with my mother the task of raising three children.

CHAPTER 3

Bialka

◆◆◆

There is in southern Poland, close to the border of the Slovak Republic, a village called Bialka. It was here that my maternal grandparents were born in 1872. The village is approximately eight miles south of Nowy Targ and about twenty miles north of Zackopane, the largest nearby towns. This part of Poland is in the Carpathian mountain range, and while there are areas of rounded hills and heavy forests, not far from Bialka some of the mountain region has alpine features of sharp peaks, steep ridges and cliff faces of bare rock. To the southwest of Bialka is High Tatra, the highest peak in Poland, 8,199 feet above sea level. The mountainous nature of the area, plus the special dialect given to the native language by the local residents, led to them being called *Goraly*, meaning mountaineers, by their countrymen.

In 1872 less than five hundred people lived in Bialka, and living conditions were primitive. A long dirt road ran through the center of the village and was the only street. On both sides of the road, houses were spaced to line up with a small plot of farm land immediately behind each house. A few families owned and farmed additional land outside the village, but the majority had single farms within the village consisting of three or four acres at most. A few farms approached ten acres in size, but they were rare. The limited acreage made it difficult to use the land for pasture purposes. As a result, animals grazed in the mountains near the village from spring until winter. The houses, made of wood, were not much more than oversized cabins with plain wooden floors. Electricity and running water were not available; oil lamps and candles provided illumination and hand dug wells were the source of water. Wood was the energy source for both heating and cooking, and gathering it from the nearby forests was continual. To provide additional warmth for the houses during the harsh winters, shelters for the farm animals connected to the back of each dwelling. In this way the heat generated by the animals helped to warm the house.

 Life in Bialka was difficult in 1872 and had been that way for many decades. The standard of living was extremely poor and prospects for improvement were all but nonexistent for most people. While children had the opportunity to attend school through the eighth grade, the needs of the farm were such that few received that level of education. For most children formal education ended in the third grade, and completing six years of education was a notable achievement. Although entire families worked together in the operation of the small farms, family income remained limited. Hard cash came from the sales of chickens, ducks, sheep, hogs, other animals and crops whose sales would not create a family hardship. For the average family, reaching even a reasonable level of living was dependent upon the full-time efforts of all members to make the small farm a success. Having a large family did much to ensure success, but it was more in terms of family survival and did not significantly raise the standard of living. In addition, a problem arose when children, males in particular, were ready to marry and wished to establish a farm of their own. The farms of the parents were often too small to divide, and the money needed to buy other land was not available.

The unfortunate history of Poland added to the complications of life in 1872. Once a great empire, one that ruled a significant part of Europe, Poland's nobles feuded and fought throughout the 17th and 18th centuries. Strong leadership and a centralized government were lacking; as a result, the country was weak and divided. Austria, Prussia and Russia took advantage of that poor political situation, and in 1792 each annexed a part of Poland. The section of Poland taken by Austria during this first partition included Bialka, whose residents immediately became subjects of the Emperor of Austria. In 1793 Prussia and Russia annexed additional sections of Poland, and in 1795 Austria joined Prussia and Russia in dividing between them all that remained of Poland. It was not until the end of World War 1 that Poland again became an independent nation.

Controlled by a foreign power, living on the edge of poverty, and having severely limited opportunities to improve their lot in life, many of the young adults in Bialka chose to go to America. Encouraged by letters from those who had gone to America earlier, and inspired by the positive terms used to describe the land, prospects for employment and especially the quality of life in this new country, many resolved to leave Bialka. Getting there, however, required a significant level of cooperation among family members to raise the capital needed to finance the passage of even one child to America. Assistance often included the hope and understanding that once their son or daughter became established in America, financial aid would flow back home on a regular basis. Others received loans from relatives or friends already in America while a few may have saved, over a long time, the funds needed for a trip that would forever change their lives.

Leaving Bialka and starting on a remarkable journey toward a better life required a certain toughness of spirit, firm resolve and courage. While the motivations for leaving were many and varied, America was thousands of miles away; it was an unfamiliar place where the primary language was not Polish and both the rules and most of the people were different. The emigrants were leaving the closeness of family and friends, a deeply religious atmosphere, and the only home they had ever known. The possibility was great that they would not return to see parents, brothers, sisters, or the land in which they were born and raised. Despite the fears that they may have felt and the emotional bonds that made leaving difficult, they left for America strengthened by the hope and faith that the opportunities available in that growing land would greatly improve the quality of their lives and ensure a promising future for their children.

CHAPTER 4

Passage to America

◆◆◆

My grandparents, Joseph Oblazney and Mary Loyack, left Bialka to begin the long journey to America in late May 1893. For reasons that are not clear, they did not know each other while growing up in Bialka, and although passengers on the same ship traveling to America, did not meet. Their first meeting would take place in the future, in Whites Crossing.

Oral history indicates they sailed to America from Gdansk, a port city in northern Poland, on the Baltic Sea. Their home in Bialka, in the extreme southern part of Poland, made the travel distance to Gdansk at least seven hundred miles. The first part of the journey from Bialka was by horse and wagon to the town of Nowy Targ. At Nowy Targ they boarded a train for Warsaw, taking with them large trunks containing their clothes and treasured possessions. From Warsaw a second train took them to Gdansk, ending the two days of travel from Bialka. It is unlikely they had ever been so far from home before, and pondering the distance and travel time remaining must have been a very sobering experience.

The ship boarded at Gdansk, believed to be the *Estonia*, was the only oceangoing passenger ship owned by Austrian-dominated Poland at that time. The *Estonia* was a steamship that, like other ships of that era, used coal to fuel the furnaces. It carried about five hundred passengers on each crossing. Being relatively poor, most of the immigrants traveled tourist class. While some fortunate passengers shared a cabin for four, most lived in dormitory-like rooms, sleeping on stacked bunk beds. Although buying food aboard ship was often possible, most emigrants brought along their own food: breads, cheese, smoked meat and other items that were slow to spoil. Separate bathroom facilities were available for men and women, but they were communal, not private. They passed time on board ship discussing plans for life in America: where they were going, what kind of work they planned to do, who would be there to welcome them and where they would live. They were also free to move about the ship, get fresh air and sun, watch the ocean and meet fellow emigrants.

> The relatively good accommodations and treatment were largely the result of laws passed by Congress in 1882 that regulated conditions on board ships bringing immigrants to the United States. It required steamship companies to provide more services and larger accommodations to passengers traveling in steerage, or tourist class. A doctor had to be available if the ship carried more than fifty passengers and an infirmary equipped to handle most emergencies was an additional requirement. Complete manifests accounting for all passengers were part of the regulations and significant fines discouraged violations, especially in situations where a passenger died in transit due to negligence. Over time the law had the impact of sharply reducing abusive practices directed toward immigrant passengers.

The ocean voyage from Gdansk began in a northwesterly direction across the Baltic Sea. The ship then sailed between

Denmark and Sweden and moved into the North Sea. Now headed in a southwesterly direction, it sailed past Germany, the Netherlands and Belgium. As the ship passed through the English Channel separating England and France, it stopped for twenty-four hours at an English port to pick up coal. From there the ship sailed west across the Atlantic Ocean. In all, the ocean voyage to America took fourteen days. For the many who suffered from ocean sickness, it was a long two weeks. The only relief from motion illness was the one-day stop in England.

As the ship moved through Upper New York Bay, it passed by the Statue of Liberty, a monument that President Grover Cleveland dedicated in 1886. For emigrant passengers on all ships, the sight of this magnificent monument to freedom was a cause for applause, dancing, singing and weeping. It symbolized that, after a long and difficult journey, they had reached the promised land; their hopes for a new beginning in life had taken a giant step toward reality. A poem written by Emma Lazarus to stimulate a fund raising drive to build the pedestal for the statue captured the spirit of the welcome extended to the immigrants. Her poem, "The New Colossus," engraved on a bronze plaque and mounted on the interior of the pedestal, eloquently expressed all that the statue represented to those following their dreams to America. In part, it read:

> Give me your tired, your poor,
> Your huddled masses yearning to breathe free,
> Send these, the homeless tempest-tost to me,
> The wretched refuse of your teeming shore,
> I lift my lamp beside the golden door.

The beauty of the Statue of Liberty and the inspiration it generated contrasted sharply with the realities met at the immigrant processing center on Ellis Island. This was the last major obstacle remaining before they proceeded to their final destination, and the possibility of being denied entry to this land of hope magnified the apprehension of the new arrivals. The main building itself was intimidating; four hundred feet long, two stories high, one hundred and fifty feet wide with a ceiling that was thirteen feet high on the first floor. Designed to process ten thousand immigrants per day, the volume of people, the noise, strange languages being spoken and the need to follow instructions barely understood was all but overwhelming for those who had spent most of their lives in a small village. Struggling with their baggage and eager to follow directions, they hurried toward the final scrutiny of their credentials and qualifications for entry to the United States.

Lined up and directed to the second floor, immigrants climbed the stairs as officials carefully observed them to detect physical impairments. Those exhibiting handicaps had to submit to closer examination to ensure the handicap would not prevent them from earning a living in the United States. Often, this resulted in the separation, at least temporarily, of family members and caused much concern. On the second floor, the immigrants moved through one of ten lines and passed before immigration agents who questioned them, checked passports, visas, documents relating to education or training, and other items that might increase their chances for acceptance into this new country. Beyond this point, they went to one of two holding pens, one for those whose destination was New York City or its suburbs and the other, holding the larger number, for those going to other states.

Ticket sellers from a variety of railroad companies were also on hand as were information clerks, a telegraph office and places to buy food. Eventually, those not detained for some reason took their baggage and boarded a government-operated steamer, one similar to a ferry boat. The steamer took them on a short trip to the wharves of railroad companies. From here they would continue their travels. At this point the immigrants had good reasons to feel relief. While they still had to reach their final destination, the main part of their long and harrowing journey to America had ended with acceptance into the United States. This was not the case for all immigrants passing through Ellis Island. Of the twenty million immigrants processed through the center before it closed in 1954, about four hundred thousand failed to gain entry.

Nearing the end of their long journey toward a new life, my grandparents, still unaware of each other, went in different directions when they left New York City. Joseph traveled to northeastern Pennsylvania to work in the coal mines and live with friends in Whites Crossing. Mary went to Chicopee, Massachusetts, drawn there by opportunities to work in the textile mills and to be with people from the Bialka area who were already there. It was June 11, 1893, their first day in America.

CHAPTER 5

The Meeting
◆◆◆

Each of my grandparents succeeded in finding work in the place they had chosen to live; she in the textile mills of Chicopee, Massachusetts and he at the Wilson Creek coal mine, about one mile from Whites Crossing. At his location it turned out that there were many more young, unmarried immigrant men than there were young women. This situation resulted in the young bachelors traveling to nearby points, such as certain towns in New Jersey, where a surplus of young, unmarried immigrant ladies lived. The object was to find a wife, one willing to return to Whites Crossing, marry, establish a home and start a family. For many couples this adventure worked out well, even though the courtship period, because of the distance involved, was often very brief.

At the time, one of the residents at Whites Crossing was Jacob Loyack, my grandmother Mary's brother. Jacob wrote numerous letters to Mary to persuade her to come to Whites Crossing to live. He emphasized the benefits of being with family, the extensive Polish community that was developing in the area, the resemblance it had to their homeland and the number of people from Bialka who lived there, many of whom she knew. In time, she agreed to leave Chicopee and go to Whites Crossing to live with Jacob and his family.

Overjoyed by this good news, Jacob planned a huge welcome party for his sister. The invitation list included many from the community and was of special interest to the bachelors living there. With few exceptions, they all prepared to make the best possible impression. This meant haircuts, trimmed beards and mustaches, serious bathing and dressing in the best clothes they had. My grandfather was one of the keenly interested bachelors. He was fairly tall, just an inch or two under six feet. He had blond hair, combed to the right, and an equally blond mustache that drooped around his upper lip and curled up at the ends. With his blue eyes, a serious demeanor and a physique that gave clear indications of great strength, he was a rather imposing figure. The lady dominating his interest and that of others was at least a head shorter than he was, possibly a few inches over five feet. Her hair was black and full around her face. She had brown eyes, high cheek bones and a fair complexion. She was slender in build and had the look of a prim and proper lady.

On the day of the welcome party, most likely a Sunday, the traditional day for celebrations, nearly all the guests had arrived before my grandfather made his appearance. When he did show up, he was balancing on his right shoulder a large keg of beer. His entry, the drink he brought to the party and the display of great physical strength got everyone's attention. He placed the keg of beer in the middle of the room and announced to one and all that Mary would be his girl and they would eventually marry.

The married couples, delighted by this dramatic turn of events, applauded and encouraged his bid to be the suitor of Mary Loyack. The other bachelors, understandably, were less supportive of this preemptive move to monopolize Mary's time and attention. They protested loudly while they sampled the beer Joseph had brought to the party. It is not clear what Mary's initial response was. Although surprised, my grandmother was obviously receptive to the bold pronouncement made by my grandfather. After a suitable courtship period, they decided to marry. Wishing to be married by a priest who spoke their language, they traveled by horse and carriage to Plymouth, about thirty miles west of Whites Crossing, and became man and wife in Saint Stephen's Church. Father Joseph Kossalko performed the ceremony on Tuesday, April 14, 1896.

The story of my grandparents' meeting, which they often confirmed, was one frequently repeated by their children. The grand entrance to the party and the confidence with which my grandfather established himself as Mary's suitor was remarkable. A display such as that did not fit the character of the grandfather we would come to know. He was soft-spoken, quiet, reserved and not given to calling attention to himself. He projected an atmosphere of calmness and strength, a man at peace with himself. As a result, the motivations for his actions are open to speculation. It is possible that, while Mary and Joseph had not formally met before the party, they knew each other by sight and name. There seems to have been a link that existed before Mary came to Whites Crossing. Whatever it was, it was clear that Joseph was not about to take the chance that someone other than he would win Mary.

Following their marriage, Joseph and Mary rented a house in Whites Crossing. It was the first house on the left on the road to Simpson, just around the corner from Billy Kresock's tavern. It was at this house that, after a series of miscarriages, their first three children were born: Annie, Mary and Lucille. In January, 1904, they bought from the estate of Patrick Kelly a house and about eight acres of land located along the Milford and Owego Turnpike, later known as Route 6. The house stood on a small rise, about eighty feet back from the road. Behind the house and to the left was a large barn, a structure that symbolized their desire to engage in farming. In this respect they, like many of their friends from Poland, were bringing some aspects of the life they had known to their new country. It was at this, the first home they owned in the new world, that two additional children, Andrew and Antoinette, were born. It was also here that they suffered a deep personal tragedy when their only son, Andrew, died at age five. In 1914 they decided to build a new home on land just to the left of their first house. Their last child, Joseph, would be born here, an event that brightened their lives considerably. This is the home that all the grandchildren would remember warmly as a special place where Joseph and Mary consistently and generously gave love, caring and the delicious ethnic foods of Poland.

CHAPTER **6**

The Irish Factor

◆◆◆

Sometime during the mid-1860s the four people who would become my father's grandparents emigrated to the United States from Ireland. All four were from County Mayo, in the northwestern part of Ireland that borders the Atlantic Ocean. They were a part of the mass migration from that land that began during the great potato famine of the 1840s. Those leaving Ireland over the next few decades were not only escaping hunger and the multitude of illnesses that accompanied that condition, they were also seeking economic security and relief from the restrictions that anti-Catholic laws had imposed for generations on Ireland's Roman Catholics. As with immigrants from other parts of Europe, their motivation was to go to this relatively new country where opportunities to work and establish a higher quality of life were abundant. That they came to America before laws governing passenger ship standards became effective in 1882 suggests the trip was difficulty and risky. It is also an indication of their intense desire to find a better life.

My paternal grandmother, Teresa, was born on June 16, 1878, in Forty Fort, Pennsylvania, a town in Luzerne County that is just north of Wilkes-Barre. Her parents were Patrick Layden and Ellen Lynett. An old newspaper article indicates her father held

Grandmother Teresa Rowland

a high position in a company called Simpson, Wathius & Company in or near Forty Fort. In 1892 the family relocated to Simpson where Patrick worked as a foreman at the Franklin Breaker, a large wood and metal structure built for processing coal into various sizes before selling it. At the time there were five children in the family, three girls and two boys, and the family lived at 30 Spencer Street in Simpson. A studio photograph taken of Grandmother Teresa in Carbondale in 1895, when she was seventeen years old, shows a strikingly beautiful girl with curly dark hair around a calm but serious face and braided hair turned up in the back to form a bun. Clear-eyed with finely sculpted features, her appearance is that of a very dignified and poised young lady. My grandfather, John, was born on October 29, 1872. There is conflicting information as to where he was born; one source indicating Kingston, Pennsylvania and a second source putting forth Girardsville, Pennsylvania as his likely birth place. Oral history within the Rowland family strongly suggests he was born in Kingston. If so, this is surprisingly close to Forty Fort, where Teresa was born. There is no evidence, however, that the families knew each other before both moved to the Carbondale/Simpson area. My grandfather's parents were Martin Rowland and Kathryn Walsh. No records on Martin Rowland's employment exist, but it is reasonable to assume he was a miner or worked in a related field. Also lost from the family history is information on brothers and sisters my grandfather may have had.

While I am certain my grandfather was the subject of many photographs over the years, only one survived. Family photo albums and other documents that might have served to give a complete history of the Rowland family burned in a house fire shortly after World War II. The photograph of my grandfather is taken from a group picture of the wedding party that celebrated the marriage of his oldest son, Patrick, to Mary Oblazney. The picture of my grandfather shows a slim man, about 5' 6" tall, possibly 140 pounds, wearing glasses and having slightly wavy black hair combed to the right. A handsome looking man, he was forty-eight years old when his son married. He had the look of a man who smiled a lot. While most of the participants in the wedding party look suitably solemn, the hint of a smile at the corners of his mouth is more clearly reflected in his eyes. The image is that of an open, friendly and happy person, one who would make a pleasant friend.

Clearly, the Layden family moved to Simpson because of a new job opportunity. The motivation for the Rowland family's

Grandfather John Rowland

move into the same area is not as obvious. Certainly, the possibility of employment had to be a factor. It may also have been a desire to be closer to family and friends. In any event, the family would have had to have been there in 1897 or 1898 because, allowing for a suitable courtship period, John and Teresa married on February 8, 1899, in Saint Rose Catholic Church in Carbondale. John was twenty-six and Teresa was twenty.

The first home for the newly married couple was in the village of Simpson. The 1900 census lists them as a family of three: John,

Teresa and their first child, Patrick. It also lists John's occupation as a coal miner and indicates that Teresa's brother and sister-in-law, Patrick and Julia, lived close by. In 1910 the family was living on Morass Avenue in Simpson and had grown dramatically. In addition to Patrick, the children included Ellen, Alice, Joseph, Marguerite and Martin. Later, the family moved to a larger home located at 723 Main Street in Simpson, about one block from Saint Michael's, the Polish Catholic Church in the community. The new location was also close to the Wilson Creek coal mine and coal yard where my grandfather worked. It was at this location that three more children, Teresa, Francis and Kitty, were born to the family. It was also at this location that they suffered a painful loss when their daughter, Teresa, died of diphtheria at age five.

About 1920 or 1921 the family moved again to a home located at number Nine 43rd Street in Carbondale. For the grandchildren this house symbolized the Rowland homestead. It was a place one looked forward to visiting because the welcome was always so warm and the hospitality so pleasant. My grandparents enjoyed having people in their home and entertaining them. When guests came calling, they quickly put everything else aside to focus attention on the visitors. This spirit of innate friendliness, caring and warmth became a family tradition that influenced all of their children. There is every indication that this was a happy, easygoing and supportive group, one that was close and loving. The family, it seems, clearly reflected the spirit, character and personality of John and Teresa.

Early in my childhood it became quite evident that grandmother Teresa was a very special lady. One of the things that impressed me greatly throughout my life was the way people who knew her well would describe her. Some were family members, others were not, but all had the same positive impression. I do not recall a single conversation about Teresa where the person did not volunteer the fact that she was exceptionally beautiful. While most of the time they were referring to her tall stature, excellent posture, dark hair and fair skin, it was obvious she impressed them even more by being the kind of person she was. My mother, in particular, was especially fond of her and often spoke of her kindness, her love of family and her generous, warm-hearted spirit. It would have been great to have known her, but my knowledge of her relies on a single photograph and the numerous stories of those who did; she died at age forty-eight, when I was barely three.

CHAPTER 7

Pat and Mary

◆◆◆

My father, Patrick, was born on October 27, 1899, most likely on Morass Avenue in Simpson, the first child of John and Teresa. As with most children of that era, his formal education was not extensive; he completed six years in elementary school. By the time he was thirteen, he worked for the Hudson Coal Company at the Wilson Creek mine and coal yard in Simpson. While he may have worked inside a coal mine at some time, there is no evidence that he did. Frequently, boys of his age picked slate from coal as it passed through a coal breaker. Eventually, he became an engineer on Oswald locomotives and retained this position for the remainder of his career with the Hudson Coal Company. The electrically powered Oswald locomotives came in different sizes. The smaller versions entered coal mines on rails and traveled to a point within the mine where coal was hand loaded into coal cars by miners. When the cars were all filled, the Oswald engineer pulled them from the mine and into the coal yard. Outside, larger Oswald locomotives shifted full and empty cars around the coal yard, delivered coal to the breaker for processing, and moved the finished product to a shipping point. Being an engineer was a choice job in an industry noted for high risk and hard labor. That my father attained this particular position at a relatively early age seems to fit well with the reputation he developed for being mechanically skilled.

My mother, Mary, was born on February 21, 1903, in Whites Crossing, the second child of Joseph and Mary. Growing up on a small family farm meant she had numerous daily chores to perform. They included feeding chickens, cows, and the family horse, gathering eggs from the hen house, tending the garden, and assisting her mother with household work. As with my father, her formal education ended with the sixth grade. For reasons that are not clear, she went to New Jersey at age thirteen to live with family friends and work in a textile mill. The most likely motivation for this was the family need for another source of income. While she did what was necessary, it was a separation that caused her considerable unhappiness. She worked in New Jersey for approximately two years. Once during this time she received a surprise visit from her mother and the baby of the family, Joseph. Delighted by the visit, she was certain they had come to take her back home, but that was not the case; it was simply a visit. Her eventual return, at age fifteen, made the entire family a lot happier. She began a new job at the textile mill in Simpson and rejoined her friends in all the social activities she had missed. The things she enjoyed most, singing and taking part in plays, led to her joining the choir at Saint Michael's Church.

At the time my mother and father met, she was living at the family homestead on Canaan Street and he was living with his parents at 723 Main Street in Simpson. My mother and her family belonged to Saint Michael's Church, the so-called Polish church in the area, and it appears the Rowland family attended mass at Saint Michael's on occasion since they lived within a block of the church. It would have been more convenient for them to go there than to travel to Saint Rose, the Irish church in Carbondale, the one listing them as registered members. It was at Saint Michael's that my mother and father met, as singers in the church choir. We really don't know how my father qualified to sing in a Polish choir. It is a fact that he did sing well, and with his lively, outgoing personality, he somehow got into the choir and learned to sing Polish hymns. He became known as the only Irish tenor in the Polish choir, a notable achievement, especially since he did not speak the language.

There is reason to believe that neither family celebrated Pat's courtship of Mary. The tendency was to encourage young adults to stay within the clan when developing a friendship that might result in marriage. The society that some were beginning to call the great melting pot because of the successful assimilation of diverse cultures had not yet earned that title. Not quite comfortable with people from entirely different backgrounds, the relatively new immigrants counseled their children to "... stay with your own kind." For the children, however, the assimilation process was underway, and they were responding to all the things that made them care deeply for a specific person without being concerned about that person's ethnic background.

As the courtship continued and grew more serious, both Pat and Mary worked hard to get parental approval to marry. One argument my mother used with her parents was Pat's determination to marry her. If they did not bless the marriage, she told them, Pat planned to "steal her away" and marry without anyone's approval. In the end, perhaps the most persuasive reasons for blessing the proposed marriage were that both young people were working, obviously dedicated to each other and very persistent in wanting to share their lives. Their persistence, no doubt, had a lot to do with finally winning over their parents.

The marriage, which took place on October 18, 1920, at Saint Michael's Church, was a very formal affair, complete with gowns, finely tailored suits, attendants and ushers. My mother's sister, Annie, was maid of honor and my father's cousin, Tommy Layden, served as best man. Lucille, a younger sister of my mother, was a bridesmaid and Cyprian Zukowski, a close neighbor and friend of the Oblazney family, was an usher. Joseph Oblazney, the youngest family member, was the ring bearer while Kitty Rowland, the youngest child in the Rowland family, was the flower girl. Father Valentine S. Matuszewski performed the marriage. My grandfather, Joseph, gave the bride in marriage and my grandfather John, it appears, did the same for his son.

Following the marriage ceremony, a reception at my grandparents' home on Canaan Street began the celebration of the wedding. It was a huge affair, attended by friends, relatives, co-workers and most of the people who lived in Whites Crossing. The formal kitchen on the main floor became a dance hall, with music furnished by a local polka band. Polish foods of all type dominated the menu, and there was no shortage of beverages. Guests gathered in the parlor, sitting room, on the front and back porches and out on the lawn. It was, by all accounts, a grand celebration, which lasted for two days. My father's parents and all of his brothers and sisters were in attendance, as were other relatives and friends of the Layden and Rowland families. None were strangers to good parties; however, the Polish food was certainly different for them. While adapting to Polish ethnic food would take more time, the melding of the different clans at this gathering was quite successful. The wedding celebration remained a very pleasant memory for the community for a long time.

A formal wedding photograph, done in the standard brown sepia tones fashionable at that time, captures the elegance of the occasion. The men look handsome, the ladies and children beautiful and all look very dignified. My parents appeared to be quite mature, even though my father was not quite twenty-one and my mother was four months short of her eighteenth birthday. He was about 5' 7," 145 pounds, with brown eyes and dark hair combed straight back. He had the look of a happy young man, but one who was taking this marriage business very seriously. My

Patrick and Mary Rowland

mother, approximately 5' 3" and not more than 115 pounds, had an unusually peaceful and composed look about her. Behind wire-framed glasses that are barely discernible in the photograph, her brown eyes have a look of one dreaming of the future. Her brunette hair, cut short, emphasized a clear, calm face. She was a very lovely bride. As with all wedding pictures, the photograph seems to stand as a symbol of hope for a long, fruitful and happy marriage.

While both my parents held jobs before their marriage, it was the custom of that time for children to contribute almost all their earnings to their parents for the benefit of the entire family. As a result, they had little savings and began their married life by living with my mother's parents. They would stay there for about three years and have two children at the home of Joseph and Mary. Marian, their first child, was born on January 19, 1922, and Patrick was born on July 27, 1923. It appears the living arrangement worked well except for one thing; my father never really adapted to Polish foods, even after three years of sampling delicacies especially prepared by my grandmother. His favorite meal was roast beef, mashed potatoes, gravy and peas, a menu that later became a standard in his own household.

By July, 1923, my parents were eager to have their own home. They were about to be a family of four, needed more space, and felt they could afford the payments associated with a small but new house. A major factor in their planning was the fact that my mother's parents offered to deed to them, for $1.00, a lot from their farm. The transfer, completed on July 10, 1923, led to the construction of a one-story bungalow within three months. My father, who had developed extensive experience as an electrician, wired the house and contributed to the building of it as his job would permit. The new home was between that of the Zukowski family and my Aunt Annie, and just two doors away from my grandparents.

The pleasure of owning a new home was considerably dampened by the fact that my sister, Marian, ill with a diabetic condition since birth, was in failing heath. Although extensive efforts to stabilize her condition continued, medical science had not yet advanced to the point where that was possible. By mid-1924 Marian was a walking, talking, blond-haired child who could express her feelings of illness and discomfort. There were also visible signs that she was extremely ill, signs that added greatly to the deepening worry and concern of my parents. The level of anxiety over Marian's failing health continued to rise for my parents and their families as the extraordinary efforts on their part and that of the medical profession failed to bring any improvement in her condition. The long struggle to restore her to good health ended when she died on July 25, 1924.

For many years after this family tragedy, those who were there to witness it would speak of it in soft and regretful tones, as if the hurtful event had occurred too recently to discuss in any other way. So it was with my mother; she would talk of Marian only infrequently, and this, I believe, was simply because the loss remained too fresh and the pain too great. It is certain that the greatest help my parents received in coping with the death of their first child was that their son, Patrick, was one year old at the time and required much of their attention. In addition, their second daughter, Ruth, was born on March 14, 1926. The new home, growing family and work demands focused the attention of my parents on positive aspects of life and, to the extent such is possible, helped to bring a measure of healing into their lives.

CHAPTER 8

View From a Front Porch

◆◆◆

The family of four was fairly well established when I arrived on July 23, 1927. For the next nine years I would be the youngest in the family, recipient of all the privileges and disadvantages inherent in that position. By the time I was old enough to be fully aware of what was going on, many of the family traditions had taken form. One that I became aware of early in life was going to church on Sunday. Of course, this was not a ritual with our small family only; it was a way of life for the entire community. Most people were careful about going to a specific ethnic church, and they went without fail every Sunday and every Holy Day. It was an event that actually began on Saturday with the traditional Saturday night bath for the children. For those old enough to receive communion, a strict fast would begin at midnight and continue until the reception of communion at one of the Sunday masses. The fasting, masses said in Latin, confessions, and the smell of incense during Lent were just a few of the many religious rituals that were a major source of strength and comfort in the deeply religious community.

On Sunday morning after breakfast we got dressed in our best "church" clothes, which we usually removed as soon as we returned home to keep them looking good. When I had to wear

Patrick and Mary, Ruth, Pat and Don Rowland

a tie, my father would fix it in place. I would stand before him frequently, my eyes even with his belt buckle, while he fashioned the knot. He smelled of tobacco, and the index and forefinger of his right hand showed the stains of nicotine from countless cigarettes. Even as he worked on my tie, more often than not, he would have a cigarette in the right corner of his mouth as he worked to get me dressed. He would hold his head tilted to the left in an effort to keep the smoke out of his eyes. I thought it very manly.

Sunday dinner always took place about noon or a little later, and my mother was an exceptional cook. Roast beef, mashed potatoes, gravy and peas were standard fare because that was what my father enjoyed the most, and it was always delicious. Occasionally, pork chops replaced the beef, but the rest of the fare remained constant. A homemade pie or cake was a part of every Sunday dinner, and there was always some remaining for later in the day. My favorite dessert was apple upside down cake. After placing a piece on a serving plate, my mother covered it with a warm sauce, an addition that made it the finest tasting dessert ever made. She enjoyed serving good food and constantly encouraged everyone at her table to "eat some more." The quality of the food made it easy to take second helpings or look forward to leftovers in the evening, at the meal we called supper. The Sunday dinner tradition, with everyone seated at the round table in our small kitchen, was really a celebration of that special day of the week. We did not realize at the time that it was also a celebration of a young family.

———◆◆◆———

Sometimes, during the summer and fall, we would go to a very early mass, return home for a quick breakfast, and get ready to go on a day trip. My mother would fill a picnic basket with a variety of food and drinks while my father made sure the car had gas and oil for a long trip. Pat, Ruth and I would get into the back seat of the family Chevrolet after storing the picnic basket in the small trunk. Our parents would take their seats up front and we would be off to Bear Mountain Park in New York State. This was a special treat, especially for us children, because we drove what appeared to us to be a very long way. Driving the fifteen miles to

Honesdale was an event in itself, but going through Wayne County and the wilds of Pike County made it seem like an adventure. Crossing into New York State and finally reaching Bear Mountain confirmed, at least in my mind, that we had accomplished something significant. A highlight of the trip was crossing the Bear Mountain Bridge, which spanned a deep gorge. Even though there was a fee for crossing, we never missed the pleasure of a slow ride across the bridge as we marveled at the sights below. We would arrive home after dark, pleasantly tired but still thinking and talking about the most memorable parts of the day.

There is something about a front porch that adds a unique and friendly atmosphere to a house, and ours, being seven steps above ground level, also provided a great view. It faced McDonald's large hay field, and we could look across those acres of grass at the forest hiding an abandoned railroad bed and a locally famous artesian well, one that steadily gushed a stream of cold, pure water. Beyond that low stretch of forest, the Moosic mountain range dominated the skyline and sheltered in one of its ravines the reservoir we called New Dam. One of the more spectacular views from our porch often came during a summer thunderstorm. The sheets of rain and the noise would become supporting characters to the lightning that danced across the mountain top. Because of its closeness and size, the mountain appeared to announce early and clearly each changing of the season and delivered the messages right to our front door.

We had a combination of at least five rockers and chairs on the porch, and when it got crowded, the children would sit on the top step while the adults took the good seats. There were always conversations going on with people walking along the road, and a lot of waving to friends driving by in cars. Many times those passing by would come up on the porch to sit, visit, and exchange news. We enjoyed listening to their conversations, even when we did not know what they were talking about. The open, lively exchanges often contained some colorful language; while we children may not have understood all the words, we seemed to adopt the language quite easily.

At times my father and a few friends would sit and talk quietly or gather around a console radio my father would bring to the porch to listen to broadcasts of championship boxing matches. All the while they smoked hand-rolled cigarettes. From pockets they pulled thin packs of cigarette papers and a pouch or flat can of tobacco, such as Bugler or Prince Albert. Holding the cigarette paper in an open fold with their left hands, they would carefully shake into the paper enough tobacco to form a cigarette. Then they licked the lightly glued edge of the paper and rolled the tobacco into a completed cigarette. When my father's cigarette burned down to the last inch, he would hand it to me with the instructions to take the butt to the kitchen and throw it into the coal stove. I was always eager to do that, but I never made the trip by going from the porch, through the house, and into the kitchen. Instead, I would go down the front steps of the porch, walk up the driveway alongside the house, and go into the kitchen by the back door. In this way I could get two or three careful puffs on the cigarette before I threw it into the stove. At the time I thought I was being very clever; it was some years before I realized my father knew what was going on and was simply enjoying the game.

When the cold weather arrived, we carried the rockers and chairs to the basement for storage. The front porch and all the activity that took place there ended for the year, and we missed it. It served as a window on the community, a way of maintaining contacts, getting news, and socializing. Even though the winter brought an end to the friendly gatherings and verbal exchanges that took place on and from the porch, it always retained its welcoming atmosphere, especially when we were coming home on a cold, dark night and the porch light was on.

Canning of food was a way of life as we were growing up in Whites Crossing. We had no refrigerator or freezer, and I do not recall any family that did. The only cold storage I was aware of was located at Fedor's and Rushen's grocery stores. As a result, it was not uncommon to come home to the aroma of spicy foods being put into sterilized jars. My mother, with Ruth's help at an early age, made catsup, chili sauce, sweet pickles, relishes and numerous jars of canned fruit such as peaches, pears, cherries and anything else that became available. The objective was to do enough canning to meet the family needs until the harvest of the following year. As we needed certain items, we simply went to the basement and brought them to the kitchen. All the really fine-tasting canned food went well with the bread baked at home at least once a week. One of the special joys of life was to get home from school at about the time a fresh batch of bread was cooling on the kitchen table. We always got to sample a slice or two, still so warm the margarine being applied melted quickly.

Making toast was something of an art since we had no toaster. First, we would remove the round lids from the top of the stove, those that covered the hot coals. If the coals were not cherry red, we opened the draft down near the ash box to make the coal burn faster. Then we poked a long fork into a slice of bread and held it over the coals, turning it at least once to get both sides brown. Sometimes we would use a grilling device that held the bread between two hinged wire mesh surfaces attached to a long handle. This kept the bread from falling onto the hot coals, and the long handle kept hands away from the heat. A favorite way of eating the toast, especially at breakfast, was with catsup or chili sauce, although toast and canned fruit also made a fine breakfast meal. The standard breakfast drink was strong, hot coffee with sugar and cream.

Occasionally, my mother or father would use our wire grill to broil pork chops or steak over the hot coals. It did not happen very often, but the aroma and taste of those special meals would linger in memory for a long, long time.

My father had a natural talent for mechanical work of all type. It seemed he could find a way to fix whatever needed repairing or built. He installed electrical wiring in houses being built by friends, constructed a garage in our backyard, at the end of the driveway, and was his own auto mechanic. Maintaining his car was probably the work he liked most because he was extremely fond of his Victoria Coupe Chevrolet. He also acquired a Model T Ford that he kept at the top of the small hill behind our house, right at the end of our lot. It was not in running order, and it was his plan to overhaul the engine and get it back on the road. While it sat idle on the hill, it was a great place for us to play, especially when the rain was beating down in a steady tattoo on the canvas roof.

When the Chevrolet required repairs, most often the work took place on a Sunday afternoon. Before the garage was constructed, work on the car took place in the open driveway. This would greatly upset Grandmother Mary, who lived just two doors away. She was an extremely pious person who firmly believed the Sabbath was holy and all had an obligation to keep it that way, especially those related to her. In her mind, working on cars was an activity not allowed on Sunday. When she would see my father doing such work, she would scold my mother for allowing such a thing to take place. My mother, in turn, would pass the message to my father, who did not take the matter too seriously. The complaints, however, finally led him to build, with the help of some friends, a one-car garage with a workshop area. The Sunday car work continued when necessary, but now it took place behind closed garage doors. I don't know if my grandmother ever realized that.

While mechanical things were a specialty with my father, he was equally at home in other areas. If my mother was working or busy attending to the children, he would clean the house, prepare meals and do some baking. While he could make great tasting cakes and pies, he considered baked bread his specialty. His style was to do these things cheerfully, often singing as he worked, a dust cloth draped from the right rear pocket of his pants.

Receiving communion for the first time was a major event for a child and his family. It usually took place when children were about eight years old, and the occasion was always a cause for celebration and picture-taking. The pictures, taken in a studio, emphasized the importance of the event, as did the new clothes, the scrubbed, wholesome look and the carefully combed hair. It was a serious, notable happening, one that seemed to mean as much to the parents and grandparents as it did to the child. First, however, the children had to demonstrate readiness for this sacrament by attending catechism classes and learning the basics of the Catholic religion.

Since the children in our family attended public school, we had to go to catechism classes at Saint Rose Church one day a week, usually in the late afternoon, for an hour of instruction. The program lasted about eight to ten weeks. Most of the other families in our neighborhood belonged to Saint Michael's Church and, since Ruth and Pat had already received first communion, I walked to classes at Saint Rose by myself, a distance of about one and a half miles. After the first few sessions, which seemed to go well, the numerous little classes scattered throughout the lower level of the church stopped their lessons one day and watched with startled apprehension the entrance of a very angry Monsignor. He demanded to know the location of a particular boy. When he found him, he yanked him out of the pew and shook him vigorously, yelling loudly all the while. I had never witnessed anything like that before; besides being scared witless, I was certain my turn was coming, something I dearly wished to avoid.

Instead of talking to my parents about my fears, and not thinking about the long-term consequences, I decided I would simply play hooky from catechism classes. The next week I left for catechism instruction as usual, but when I got within a few blocks of the church I placed the slim, four-page catechism booklet under my sweater, turned down Salem Avenue toward Main Street and went into the Newberry Store. For the next hour I carefully examined the toys, candy counter, and the leather boots for boys that we called Hi-Cuts. I admired them greatly since the right boot had a pouch near the top that contained a pocket knife. I mentally selected all the things I would buy if I had the money to do so. Occasionally, a clerk would approach and look at me suspiciously, and I would move on to another counter. When the hour was up, I walked back home.

The next week I again headed for catechism class but went instead to the Newberry Store to spend another hour looking over the merchandise. This time the clerks seemed to watch me with a higher level of suspicion, or so it appeared. After wandering about the store for about forty-five minutes, I was about twenty-five feet from the front double doors when they suddenly swung open and two Sisters from Saint Rose came walking in briskly. Dressed in black habits with starched white cloth framing their faces, they rapidly closed the distance between us while I watched in absolute terror. I was certain they knew of my plan to skip catechism class, they were coming to get me, and I would soon be face to face with the Monsignor. While my inclination was to run, I seemed anchored to the floor, waiting for the worst to happen. Then, an incredible thing took place. When they reached me, they walked right by, smiling as they talked to each other.

Greatly relieved by my good fortune, I moved quickly to get out of the store and put as much distance as possible between the Sisters and myself. As I hurried out the Main Street entrance, I noticed a long line of cars stopped in front of the store. A black car with red wire wheels was right before me. As I was thinking the car looks like ours, I looked up at the driver and into the eyes of my father; he was motioning to me to get into the car. My brief career as a hooky player was about to end.

By the time we were halfway up Canaan Street hill on our way home, my father heard the tearful story of my catechism problem. He listened calmly and told me not to worry because he thought the situation was not beyond fixing. When we got home and my mother became aware of the matter, she was equally supportive, although absolutely appalled at the thought that her youngest child faced being expelled from catechism class. A greater concern was the impact such a disgrace would have on Grandmother Mary. Intensely religious, her role in her extended family was to make certain each grandchild received each of the early sacraments of the Church. My parents resolved the issue through a discussion with the Monsignor and the Sister in charge of training. I returned to catechism classes, paid close attention to the Sisters and tried hard to be a fair student of religion as I carefully watched for any appearance by the Monsignor. I received communion with my class and I don't think my grandmother ever knew how close I had come to missing that event.

My brother, Pat, was about four years old when I was born. The age difference made it difficult for us to be playmates when we were children because I was too young for his games and activities and he was too old for mine. As the oldest child in the family, he was in a unique position. Being the first son, bearing his father's name and having significant intelligence enhanced his position even more. He was, in all respects, the older brother, one who stayed up later, experienced things first, and set the pace for Ruth and me, from school attendance to communion, confirmation and young adulthood. In many ways he seemed to us to be a smaller version of the adults in the family.

A picture of Pat taken when he was in the third grade shows an alert young boy in a white shirt and black trousers. Hair parted to the right above large eyes, he appears to be smiling slightly, as if pleased about something. In photographs where Ruth, Pat and I appear together as children, he was at least a head taller than we were and gave the impression of being the in-charge older brother. While the age difference in those early years may have been too great for us to be playmates, family circumstances would soon have us working together closely on a variety of activities, a situation that started a bonding process that never ended.

My sister Ruth was a year and four months older than I and, while we may have played together on occasion, we naturally had

Don, Ruth, and Pat Rowland

different interests. I was fond of playing "Cowboys and Indians" while she had her dolls. She also liked helping her mother with baking, cooking, and household chores. She was, in all ways, a little lady, one who became locally famous for the beauty of her hair. Her hair was dark, shoulder length and arranged by my mother in a series of long hanging curls that circled her head. The cascading curls surrounding a round face that featured large brown eyes gave her a very distinctive and attractive appearance.

Everybody, it seemed, knew Ruth because of her unusually beautiful hair. While the attention may have pleased her considerably, I suspect it pleased my mother even more.

Ruth's innate sensitivity matched her good looks. She was a natural born care-giver, a person concerned about the welfare of all family members, a young mother to everyone. This level of caring brings with it equal amounts of worry and concern, often when neither is warranted. She accepted her role with considerable grace, however, and she, like Pat, would be a major source of strength during times of adversity.

Thanksgiving and Christmas brought a glow to the family that would begin about the middle of November and last through the end of the year. As Thanksgiving approached I would carefully look through all the newspapers I could find for ads that featured drawings related to the holiday. With great care I would cut out the turkeys, especially those that had tail feathers fanned, Pilgrims going hunting in snow-covered fields and Pilgrims and Indians enjoying a Thanksgiving meal. As the treasure of drawings grew larger, I had feelings of regret that I had been born much too late to experience the noble life of the early settlers in New England. I was certain that I should have been one of them.

One year, the day before Thanksgiving, a fierce snowstorm moved into northeastern Pennsylvania. The snow was deep and blown into drifts by a strong, endless wind. To look outside through the frosted windows, we had to heat a spot on the glass by blowing on it until the frost melted. Then we rubbed the spot clear to watch the snow piling up, the drifts building, and the lack of traffic or people traveling on the road. It was a fine snowstorm.

My mother was baking and preparing food for the celebration that would take place the following day. When she announced she needed additional groceries and baking supplies from Fedor's store, I was quick to volunteer to go. It took a lot of convincing before she agreed to let me make the trip. While she prepared a list of the things needed, I was putting on heavy winter clothing, boots, scarf, hat and gloves. Although the distance to Fedor's was barely a half mile, it appeared I was preparing to walk across most of Lackawanna County.

Taking the family sled from the back porch, I moved down the driveway toward the road. My first encounter with the sharp, cold wind and driving snow caused me to have second thoughts, at least briefly, about my venture. Once on the road, with the wind at my back, the storm did not seem quite so bad. Pulling the sled through the tracks made by cars and trucks that had come through much earlier, I made my way toward Whites Crossing. The lane leading to the village from the main road was especially heavy with snow because less traffic had passed that way. The limbs of chestnut and maple trees lining both sides of the lane sagged low to form a snowy tunnel. The fact that no cars passed by and I saw no one as I trudged along created a sense of isolation that was rather nice.

When I arrived at Fedor's store I parked the sled on the snow-covered concrete slab that extended across the front of the building. Clearing the snow from my boots and clothes as best I could, I went inside to present my mother's shopping list. After a warm welcome and comments about my snowman appearance, Mr. Fedor packed the groceries into a box and provided some cord for tying the box to the sled. Heading back home into the wind made it necessary to pull the scarf across my face so that only the eyes remained uncovered. The return trip had the same sense of solitude and isolation that I encountered on the way to the store. Reaching the back porch and delivering the box of Thanksgiving groceries made that particular holiday adventure especially memorable. It also provided a keen sense of kinship with the Pilgrims of long ago.

The Christmas season always created a certain feeling of awe because of the great emphasis that our community placed on the religious aspects of that holiday. There was a feeling that the pace of life became slower and quieter and people more thoughtful and pleasant. The atmosphere of happy expectation increased significantly as that holy day grew near. It was as if the preceding months of the year were simply a preparation for this day and everyone was getting ready to focus on each aspect of the holiday, intent on treasuring every detail of happiness and goodwill until Christmas came again.

From early December my newspaper cutouts consisted of nativity scenes, Santa Claus, his elves and reindeer, decorated Christmas trees and certain toys. Pat, Ruth and I understood that each of us might get one toy, but it was just as likely we might get a toy to share. It didn't matter; whatever we got would please and elate us. We did have individual stockings to hang on door knobs, however. The stocking was always the best and longest from our stocking drawer, a real everyday stocking, the kind that fit to just below the knee. The only small concern I had was selecting the most visible knob to hang it on.

On Christmas Eve we usually awoke to the smell of something being baked. The early part of the day seemed filled with taking care of final details and getting ready for the magical atmosphere of the evening just ahead. By late afternoon we had finished bathing and got dressed for a traditional Polish Christmas Eve supper. Since it was a fast day, meaning no meat served, the meal consisted of fish, *pierogi*, cabbage and peas, *kolutz* and bread. Before the meal we would break bread with each other using a wafer-thin piece of blessed bread called *oplatek*. Every person taking part in the meal would share a small piece of his *oplatek* with everyone else, a gesture that conveyed without words love, peace and goodwill. In the home of our grandparents Joseph and Mary, an additional tradition brought from Bialka included the placing of straw in the center of the supper table to symbolize a place of welcome for the Christ child. The traditions and rituals practiced by our elders and the solemnity given to Christmas added a beauty and mystery to the holiday that passing years have not diminished.

When we went to bed on Christmas Eve in those very early years, no decorated Christmas tree stood in the house. Only table, wall and window decorations, plus the stockings hanging on the door knobs, signified it was the Christmas season. Our hope and expectations were that a tree would stand among the gifts we found in the morning. Once in bed I would try hard to be still and remain awake in the hopes of hearing Santa Claus arrive. It never worked. Usually, one of us would awake about five in the morning, before any hint of sun began to filter through the dark winter night, and look for signs of Christmas Day. The glow of colored lights seen through the cracks around the edge of the bedroom door gave a clear indication that something wonderful had happened while we slept. As we moved quietly and cautiously from the bedroom, the first sight of the fully decorated and lighted tree standing in the parlor overwhelmed us. The beauty of the tree would have been enough, but arranged around it were presents and every stocking sagged under the weight of oranges, nuts, some candy and a few coins. The wonder of Christmas morning had happened once again.

Instinctively, we would rush to our parents' bedroom, right off the parlor, to spread the good news on what we'd discovered. They played their part very well; feigning sleepiness and surprise as we pointed out the beauty of the tree and the magnificence of the gifts. Eventually, I learned how these Christmas miracles occurred, and I marveled that they could accomplish so much while we slept, giving up most of a night's sleep so we might experience a very special joy.

The Christmas season of 1935 brought a special gift into our household when a baby boy arrived in the early morning hours of January 1, 1936. This added high excitement to the season, especially since he was the first baby born in the Carbondale area that year. That honor meant publicity in the local newspapers, and based on local custom, numerous gifts for my parents and the baby from merchants in Carbondale. As with most births at the time, the baby was born at home. I recall standing at the foot of the bed the day after his birth and being amazed at his small size and tiny features. He sounded lively, and it was obvious that my parents treasured the holiday gift this child represented. He made me happy for another reason: his birth meant I was no longer the youngest in the family.

Perhaps a week following his birth, on a day when my mother's parents and other relatives gathered at our home to see the baby, a discussion began regarding the baby's name. My choice for his name was Timothy, and I argued strongly in favor of it. I don't recall why the name came to mind or why I defended my choice with such vigor. While my recommendation for a name lost, all the grownups present enjoyed my participation immensely. The name chosen for the baby was Eugene and, from that day on, I became known as Tim or Timmy. It is unlikely that any of my Whites Crossing peers would recognize me by any other name.

Gene Rowland

It was a unique experience having Gene come into our family when he did. There was a gap of almost nine years between my birth and his, and even larger gaps in age between Ruth, Pat and him. The age difference seemed to make him the child of all of us, and for a long time our attention focused on his welfare, growth and development as a small person. Over the years we took turns watching him, feeding him, dressing him, taking him outdoors in a carriage and playing with him. We watched him grow into a handsome, blond-haired boy with large brown eyes and a crooked smile that never quit, even while being chastised. He was a very pleasant and likable child, but one who too soon was left behind by his siblings simply because we reached young adulthood and moved into new responsibilities while he was yet a youngster. Still, none of us, it seems, ever stopped feeling a kind of parental kinship to this young brother who came so late into our lives.

CHAPTER 9

Babkee and Jadkee

◆◆◆

*I*n the language of Bialka, Poland, *Babka* was the affectionate term for grandmother and *Dziadek* was the word for grandfather. Sometime before I was born, the older grandchildren had difficulty with those Polish words. As a result, *Babka* and *Dziadek* became *Babkee* and *Jadkee*. Over the years this was how they became known not only to their grandchildren, but to children of other relatives, neighborhood children, and many grownups as well. The anglicized version of their Polish titles always retained the affectionate intent of the original words and conveyed a high level of respect. They were Babkee and Jadkee to almost everyone who knew them, and it seemed to fit them very well.

As a young boy I used to think that all children had grandparents who lived just two doors away. It seemed normal, natural and the way things ought to be. I don't recall when I first started to walk to their house by myself, but I suspect it must have been very early in life because it was always so pleasant to be there. A warm welcome was just the start of many happy visits. Next came a persistent encouragement to have something to eat, an offer I rarely refused. Sour rye bread with butter and a cool glass of tea was a favorite of mine, and it was here I first enjoyed specially

Grandparents Joseph and Mary Oblazney

prepared rabbit, squirrel and fish caught by my uncle Joseph during the hunting or fishing season. My grandmother enjoyed feeding people, especially her grandchildren, and we relished the variety of ethnic foods, the aroma that filled the kitchen, and the distinctive flavor of the dishes she prepared. While neither grandparent was comfortable with the English language, their actions, supported by a mixture of Polish and English words, plainly expressed the warmth of the caring they had for us.

The home of my grandparents was an L-shaped two-story house with the long stem of the L facing the road while the shorter section was further back and faced right. Built into a sloping lot, most of the basement under the larger section remained exposed. It was here that they placed their everyday kitchen. Windows on the front and left side of this kitchen made for a light and airy atmosphere. As we entered the kitchen through an outside door centered on the front of the room, there was a sink immediately to the right, between the entrance and the right wall. On that wall, close to the sink, a doorway led to a part of the basement we called the cellar. Also near that doorway was a stairway to the second floor. In the far right corner of the basement kitchen stood a coal stove used for heating and cooking. Near the stove was a doorway that opened into a large room back of the kitchen. Then, in the far left corner of the kitchen was a walk-in pantry, close to a long table that extended along the left wall. Against the wall was a wooden bench. In the left near corner was a hutch for the storage of dishes.

The room to the rear of the kitchen was basically a storage area, with clothing and other items placed in huge pieces of furniture called chifforobes, a combination of a wardrobe and a chest of drawers. The room made a great place for playing while the grownups visited in the kitchen. Besides being fairly large, it contained a coal-fired furnace on the right side of the room. During the winter months that heating plant made the room warm and cozy. The separated part of the basement, called the cellar, contained shelving for canned foods and served as a laundry room. It seemed to stay consistently cool and made a perfect place to keep sweetened tea during the hot summer months.

On the main floor, at the left front of the building, was a formal parlor. To the rear of the parlor was a sitting room; to the right of this room was a large kitchen with two pantries. It was much like a formal dining room and used only for special occasions. Even then, cooking took place in the basement kitchen and the food was carried to the first floor for serving. A front porch extended around the entire front of the house, following the L design of the structure. Another porch was at the rear of the house, matching the formal kitchen in length.

The second floor contained three bedrooms, two walk-in closets and one smaller closet. As with most homes at that time and place, there was no bathroom in the house. A large outhouse stood to the left and rear of the home, about two hundred feet from the back door. Other buildings to the rear of the house included a multipurpose shed that stored coal, mining tools, wheelbarrows and gardening implements. Just beyond the shed was a fenced-in garden area of substantial size. It contained a black cherry tree, flowers, herbs and areas for growing vegetables. To the left of the garden was a large grape arbor, and at the rear was a chicken coop and fenced-in chicken yard. The last building, to the right and about seventy feet from the garden, was a two-story barn, a large unpainted structure that had turned a weathered gray. Here my grandfather kept a few head of cattle, a horse, stored hay in the second story loft, and farming equipment on the first level. It symbolized his love for farming as well as a direct link to the life he had known as a young man in the village of Bialka, Poland, a place that he always remembered fondly.

Beyond the buildings were the fields of the farm, some used for growing corn and potatoes, but most were used to grow hay. They extended back over a rise we called the butley and followed the rear property lines of the lots along the main road that my grandparents had deeded to their children or sold to good friends. For the grandchildren, the farm was a place that offered countless opportunities to explore. We roamed the fields, fed the chickens, collected eggs from the nests, picked black cherries from the tree, dug up potatoes, picked corn, chased a hog that escaped the pen, gathered wood for the smokehouse, and stood back at a safe distance as my grandfather extracted honeycombs from the beehives. When we played hide and seek, there were many places to hide and not be found. The fields and the white birch trees beyond the farm provided numerous secluded areas for playing our favorite games. More than a place to play, the entire area provided a sense of adventure and the comfortable feeling that we were home, no matter where we were in the neighborhood at any particular time. As I grew older I came to understand that my grandparents were responsible for the special quality of where we lived. They were the patriarchs of the families clustered around their homestead, and it was their innate decency and dignity that set the standards for the kind of neighborhood we would have.

My grandmother was a small, high-strung bundle of energy while my grandfather was tall, strong and stoical. She could get excited over many things while he remained fairly calm. They were both very religious, but she was much more intensely involved in her religion. For many years she walked to Saint Michael's Church in Simpson every day to attend mass, a distance of one and a half miles each way. The distance might not seem excessive, but most of the return trip home was up a steep hill called Morass Avenue. Once, during the winter, she fell on ice and broke an arm, an event that did nothing to alter her church-going habit. Her devout practices were a legacy of her formative years in Bialka. Each year she would join a group from her village in a pilgrimage to Czestochowa, a distance of roughly one hundred and fifteen miles, to visit the shrine of the Black Madonna of Czestochowa. They walked the entire distance.

My grandfather was sincere in his religious beliefs, but he followed the more traditional practice of going to mass only on Sundays and Holy Days. He would, however, join my grandmother in observing all the customs and rituals of the church, all of which he helped to pass on to their children. One of their personal rituals was the singing of hymns on Sunday afternoons. They would harmonize earnestly in their native language through a series of hymns, and the sincerity of their private worship abundantly offset what they lacked in vocal skills.

Without question, the six-week Lenten period ending on Holy Saturday was the religious highlight of the year. For my grandparents, this was a very solemn time, one taken very seriously. The emphasis was on prayer, penance, reconciliation and reflection. The tone they projected had a quiet, somber quality that grandchildren, filled with normal youthful exuberance, had a hard time grasping. In their home during Lent the radio remained silent, a condition also encouraged for those wanting to sing. Play that generated too much laughter drew a frown, as did the chewing of gum or idly swinging our legs while seated at the table eating. Such activity while eating caused the "devil to dance on your plate." In many respects, the religious atmosphere reflected my grandmother's complex personality. Though she would laugh at jokes and stories, she would soon become quite serious, as if it was not proper, for reasons associated with religion, to be too happy. None of this detracted from her basic goodness or love for family; it just put a limit on how much happiness she would allow herself. My grandfather did not feel the same restraints. Though a quiet, calm, reflective man, he enjoyed the good times in life wherever he found them.

During Holy Week my grandparents and most of their friends attended services at Saint Michael's every day. Our family usually started the Easter week worship on Thursday, at Saint Rose Church. The most intense service was always on Good Friday, no matter which Catholic church people attended. The service, which began at noon and lasted for three hours, paralleled, we believed, the exact time of the Crucifixion. For many of us children, it was the longest three hours we ever lived through. If, for some reason, we were at home and not attending the Good Friday service, everything came to a stop at noon and remained that way until three o'clock in the afternoon. Even stores and banks closed for that three-hour period. The intent was to focus on what had taken place on that particular day and time and the impact it had on our lives.

On the Saturday before Easter, it was the custom for families attending Saint Michael's to take a basket of food to the church. There, in a special ceremony, a priest blessed the food. Included in the basket was bread, hard-boiled eggs, a special Easter sausage, horseradish, ham and perhaps an assortment of seasonings. My grandmother would prepare a large basket of food, cover it with a white cloth and give it to my grandfather to take to the church. By the time he reached Whites Crossing, many friends joined him in the walk to Saint Michael's and back with the blessed food. On Easter morning we attended the earliest mass of the day, at six o'clock. After returning home from the service, my grandfather would cut up the blessed food into fine pieces, place it in a large bowl, season it and pour buttermilk over it. Dipped into soup bowls and reverently served, this unique first meal of Easter was a tradition we greatly enjoyed. Besides being quite tasty, it symbolized a new beginning for the religious year ahead and seemed a fitting ending to the Lenten period. It was the only time of the year my grandparents served such a meal, which added greatly to the meaning it gave to Easter morning.

Like most men in the Whites Crossing area, my grandfather worked at the Wilson Creek mine, just outside Simpson. This was the first and only job he had held since coming to America, and there is reason to believe he became quite skilled at mining since later in life he discovered coal on his property and developed his own personal mine. All evidence indicates, however, that his first love was farming, the life he had known in his native country. In the new land, mining provided the resources that permitted my grandmother and him to farm, at least on a small scale, and to reproduce in America a part of their Bialka heritage.

Most of the time they had at least two cows that provided them with milk for drinking and for turning into butter and cheese. My mother often spoke of churning milk to produce the butter and cheese. It was a chore repeated over and over, one that all the children tried to avoid. While churning, they asked frequently if the product had reached the desired texture and consistency. The standard response from my grandparents was, "Just a little longer." While I do not recall taking part in the churning activity, I remember vividly the many times we would go to the barn with our grandfather for the evening milking of the cows. Cup in hand, we would watch the milking take place and wait for him to call us closer to get our cups filled with fresh milk. It was warm, sweet and probably the best thing we had ever tasted. Then we would help feed the cows by filling the hay mow with hay that had been hand cut in the fields using a sickle. Most likely we got in my grandfather's way and hampered his work at times, but he always remained composed and soft-spoken and seemed to enjoy this evening ritual.

They usually raised a hog or two for meat, and one of the big events of the fall, about mid-November, took place at butchering time. This was an all-day affair and always included friends who were skilled in the art of turning the hog into a variety of meats. A huge outdoor fire heated water that eventually filled a wooden trough. The hot water helped to remove the bristles from the hide of the slaughtered hog. The fire, smoke and activity generated a festive air, as did the lunch served by the women present. By mid-afternoon the meat was a combination of hams, bacon, chops and pork roasts. The smaller meat parts became the main ingredients for making a spiced sausage called *kielbasa*. The *kielbasa*, bacon, and hams soon hung in a smokehouse for curing. The smokehouse, about five feet square, stood on a small incline to the rear and right of the garden. It was approximately seven feet high and made from rough cut wood, each piece still having bark that faced to the outside. The top, which angled down from front to back, had similar wood, as did the door on the front. A small space between the attached boards allowed some of the smoke to escape. In the center of the earthen floor, terra-cotta piping curved underground and extended about six feet out to the front of the smokehouse and ended in a fire pit. The fire, usually of hickory wood, created the smoke that traveled through the piping and filled the small shed. Over time, the heat and smoke cured the sausage, bacon, and hams hanging near the top of the smokehouse. The finished products had a distinctive smoky flavor and were delicious.

 As I grew a bit older and became more prone to mischief, I discovered one year that the smokehouse had some loose boards on the rear wall. This led a few of us to "borrow" a sausage from the smokehouse and some potatoes from the potato patch. We built a fire at the far edge of the farm, roasted the potatoes in the hot coals until they were charcoal black on the outside and steamy white inside. Cutting the sausage into short lengths, we placed it on sharply pointed sticks for cooking over the fire. It was a great feast followed by an even greater guilty conscience. Within a few days I was helping to nail the loose boards back in place, forever retired as a raider of smokehouses.

◆◼◆

In all, my grandfather spent about thirty-seven years working in the coal mine at Wilson Creek. When he was fifty-eight he had to retire, long before he was ready or willing to do so. Two injuries led to this forced retirement. The first was the result of an incident with a bull. Among the cattle he raised was a bull that seemed to be fairly calm and domesticated. For a long time my grandfather worked around the bull without incident. One day, within the cattle yard next to the barn, and for reasons never determined, the bull attacked my grandfather and caused a severe head injury. While he recovered without any outward signs of the accident, he would periodically go into a trance-like state for brief periods. During these episodes, he seemed to have no awareness of where he was or what he was doing; he was in a world of his own and was likely to act on whatever impulses motivated him at the time. He might arise from bed in the middle of the night and begin to dress for work or return to the barn to feed cattle just recently fed. The incidents we called "spells" did not last long; once they were over, he looked tired and remained quiet. A major concern was that he might harm himself by undertaking some hazardous chore he should not attempt while in that condition. His doctor indicated he had suffered an injury to the brain and there was no way to control the periodic seizures.

An accident within a private mine he was developing on his property compounded his medical situation. A pipe, one most likely used to pump water from the mine, suddenly broke, hit his head, and caused a fracture. Again, he recovered nicely, with no outward signs of the accident. While episodes of unawareness or confusion did not occur any more frequently, they did become a concern for his employers. They concluded, with understandable justification, that his condition added a significant risk to an occupation already known for its high level of danger. It was, in their judgment, in his best interest and that of his fellow miners that he retire. He stopped working at Wilson Creek, but it was not in his nature to retire. He always felt there were coal deposits on his small farm and he continued to develop his mine in a place on his property that would not affect his farming. His intention was to find a vein of coal and use the mine to supply his needs and those of his children. Working mostly by himself, he produced coal from the mine within eighteen months. The discovery of a vein of anthracite about five feet in height pleased him greatly. While his affliction continued on an infrequent basis, he opened his private mine without incident, at least none that came to the attention of the family.

It was my grandfather's procedure to take coal from his mine in huge chunks and transport them to the coal shed at the rear of his home. Here he would stack it as high as he could reach, and, as needed for fuel, crack it into smaller pieces, place it into large buckets, and store them next to the furnace for burning. One day he was working at the coal shed, and just as my grandmother came out the back door, he suffered a spell. When she saw what was happening, she cried out for help while she tried to control him and lead him into the house. In his confused state, he obviously felt he was working in a mine. Regarding my grandmother as a timber, he lifted her high overhead with both hands and attempted to place her on top of the stacked coal, much as he would do in a mine to shore up the roof against rock and dirt falls. Someone came to her assistance and got my grandfather to put her down. Except for a few scratches and bruises, the incident ended without harm. While there was a bit of humor in what had taken place, it also emphasized that the spells affecting my grandfather had a potential for causing some hurt, either to himself or others.

Though all of his grandchildren were aware of the spells and the effects they had on him, none wanted to miss being in his company. He was still Jadkee, our strong, soft-spoken grandfather, a man who drew us to him without any apparent effort. There was no question, however, about our concern for him, and we found the spells more than a little frightening when they occurred. Still, I never anticipated having to personally deal with such an episode.

One warm spring day, when I was about eight years old, I was helping my grandparents with some yard work. A low hedge bordered the well-kept lawn to the right of their home. While my grandfather prepared a flower bed for planting, I was helping my grandmother to remove the leaves and debris that had lodged at the base of the hedge over the winter months. We had worked and talked for over an hour when my grandmother looked over at my grandfather because he had not responded to her last remark. He was kneeling at the edge of the flower bed, hands on his knees, staring toward the garden. He was having a spell. My grandmother began to wail and call for help while I stood there stunned and thoroughly frightened. Then, she urgently told me, using a mixture of English and Polish, to grab my grandfather from behind to keep him from getting up. Her thought was that, if he couldn't get up, he would not put himself in any danger. I understood her perfectly, but my fear increased tenfold when I realized what she wanted me to do. Her frantic urging and the deep personal sense that I had to do something finally got me moving. While he was still kneeling on the ground, I jumped upon his back and wrapped my arms around his neck. Though I weighed about sixty pounds, he suddenly got up, not at all hampered by the burden he was carrying, and began to walk in the direction of his mine. Hanging on grimly while my grandmother raised the volume of her cries for help, I knew I could not stop him from going into the mine and I was equally certain that I could not go in there with him. It became a question of how long I could hold on before I let go and still feel I had done all I could. The arrival of my uncle Joseph, who persuaded him to return home, kept me from finding where on the approach to the mine the critical personal test would have come.

As with all the other spells that he had over the years, I doubt that my grandfather had any recollection of that particular one. It didn't matter. I had shared a very small part in one incident and it had the impact of drawing me even closer to him. My affection for him became tinged with a touch of sadness because of his affliction, one he handled with grace and dignity. It just never seemed right, and it took me a long time to accept the fact that that was the way it was, and there was nothing anyone could do about it.

In 1918 a highly contagious flu virus swept the country, infecting a large part of the population and causing thousands of deaths. Whites Crossing was not immune from the virus. Among those who became ill were Joseph and Ann Novobilski who lived at the crossroads in the village, on the road toward Simpson. Joseph Novobilski was a distant relative of my grandfather and always addressed him as uncle. Joseph and Ann contracted the flu at about the same time and within days at least two of their five children were also ill. Joseph died from his illness on a Tuesday in November, and his wife died on the following Tuesday. For the next few weeks, while a relative of Ann cared for the children, lengthy discussions took place on their long-term care. When it became obvious that some relatives and friends of the family did not have the resources to take the children, and others simply did not want this huge burden, my grandfather decided he would take them all. My grandmother voiced some reluctance about suddenly doubling the size of her family, but she agreed that was the best of all choices. Soon she was nursing the sick children on a full-time basis.

The room in back of their basement kitchen became a bedroom for the two oldest Novobilski children, both boys, while two girls shared space with my grandparents' daughters in a crowded bedroom. The youngest Novobilski child, Barney, was just a baby at the time and slept in a crib in my grandparents' bedroom. The oldest children, Joe and Frank, were in their teens when they came to live with my grandparents; after a few years, they found jobs and left to begin life on their own. The sisters, Alice and Ann, stayed with my grandparents for at least ten years, with Alice becoming a bride and having her reception at my grandparents' home. Barney lived there until he was in his early twenties.

Except for Barney, I have no recollection of the Novobilski children living with my grandparents; much of that particular time in the life of my grandparents took place before I was born. One of the notable things that happened while the older boys were there took place when my grandfather suffered an attack by his bull. Frank happened to be nearby when the bull began the assault. Shouting to distract the bull, he grabbed a long, heavy club and began to hit the bull sharply while urging my grandfather to escape. He kept striking the bull until my grandfather, although injured, was safe. In a matter of minutes Frank had, in an unexpected way, rewarded my grandparents for their kindness to him, his brothers and sisters. From my grandparents' perspective, I doubt that they ever sought or expected any reward for their decision to shelter the Novobilski children in their home. For them it was simply the right thing to do.

One of the things my grandfather enjoyed immensely was smoking a corn cob pipe. The pleasure he got from it was always apparent since he seemed to be in a contented and reflective mood as he smoked, completely lost in his thoughts. He ordered his tobacco from a distributor who mailed it to him in the form of dried tobacco leaves. The arrival of a new bundle of tobacco leaves, especially during the warm weather, would draw many of us to his back porch. Here, using a sharp knife and a wooden cutting board, he would methodically cut the tobacco into fine pieces, taking care to remove the heavier veins from the leaves as he worked. As a pile of cut tobacco grew, he transferred it to a large crock that served as a humidor. The last step in the process was mixing the finely cut tobacco within the jar to achieve a blend from the different leaves. We would watch this in fascination, waiting for the supreme test, the lighting of the first full pipe of tobacco from this new batch. He would carefully fill his pipe as we stood smiling in anticipation. Once lit, he would puff on the pipe and slowly exhale, tasting the quality of tobacco. Then, he would smile slightly, give an affirmative nod of his head and pronounce in Polish that the batch was *dobry*, good. From our response a stranger would have thought we were a significant factor in producing the good results.

Inside the house my grandfather smoked only under very controlled conditions. My grandmother was allergic to tobacco smoke, and even a mild exposure caused severe coughing. As a result, it became my grandfather's habit, usually in the evening after supper, to smoke in the room back of the basement kitchen, close to the furnace. He did this by opening up the firebox of the furnace, which was about three feet from the base of the heating plant, and blew the smoke from his pipe into the firebox and up the chimney. It worked out well; he could smoke inside, especially when the weather was bad, with no harm to my grandmother.

Just about every grandchild, plus children of relatives and friends, experienced the pleasure of sitting with Jadkee while he smoked his pipe. The only one I am aware of who occasionally smoked with him was my brother, Pat. Jadkee fashioned a corn cob pipe for Pat one day and allowed him to sample his tobacco blend as they sat together by the furnace. I never had that opportunity, but it is one I would not have passed up. Not smoking, however, did not minimize the good feelings that came from just being there.

    Only the soft light that filtered in from the kitchen and the cherry glow of the coal burning in the furnace filled the dimly lit room. My grandfather sat in his padded kitchen chair while I sat next to him, on a short stool. Being there alone with my grandfather on a cold fall or winter evening brought about an uncommon level of closeness and comfort. There was never an extensive conversation; it was not necessary and would have detracted from the peacefulness of the moment. We would sit there silently, his face reflecting the glow from the fire, which made his curled mustache look a bit fierce as he smoked slowly and thoughtfully. I often wondered if his thoughts took him back to the home of his youth and the family and friends remaining there. I never knew; he didn't say. Always before I was ready to do so, it would be time for me to return home. As I would stand up to leave, I would say, "I've got to go now, Jadkee." He would turn, look at me, place a hand on my head or shoulder and say in his distinctive English, "You good boy, Donyell." It was like a benediction.

By 1932 almost forty years had passed since my grandparents landed at Ellis Island and began a new life in the United States. Starting with a minimum of assets but inspired to make the most of this great opportunity, they persevered through difficult times, worked extremely hard and accomplished much during those first forty years. They succeeded in establishing a very pleasant farm and transplanted many of the traditions and customs from their past to their new home. Six children were born to them, and all but one survived childhood. Part of their farm they deeded to their children and, in the process, set up a unique family neighborhood, of which they were the center. My grandfather's career as a miner had been quite successful and enabled them to attain a comfortable life for the entire family. They lived in an area with people who shared their background, culture and religion as well as their hopes for the future. In the process they developed many close, personal friendships. In 1906 they became citizens of the United States, with my grandfather renouncing "all allegiance and fidelity to the Emperor of Austria." By any measure, they attained and exceeded the dreams that had inspired them to come to this country.

Along the way, they met with some of the harsh realities of life that come when least expected, the kind of things that test the character as well as the spirit. Losing their first son, Andrew, was such an event, as was the flu epidemic that led to the doubling of the size of their family. Having to retire from mining before he was ready was a major blow for my grandfather, and the spells occurring as the result of his injuries were difficult, both for him and those who watched over him. He also tried, after retirement, to expand the scope of the mine he had established on his farm. In partnership with a son-in-law, they hired people to increase the size of the pit leading to his mine, erected a breaker to process coal and even bought a truck for the new business. Almost all the investments came from my grandparents' assets. Before the venture could turn a profit, he ran out of capital and the budding company collapsed.

An event that caused much hurt took place during Holy Week in 1932. Somehow, the two-story barn with the weathered gray wood caught fire and burned to the ground. Pulled from the burning barn were farm equipment and a few tools. Most of the animals survived the blaze, but two cows suffered burns, one so badly it could not survive. After being given much care and attention, the other, Blacky, recovered. The loss was devastating to my grandparents, especially my grandfather; he thought he might have caused the fire by leaving a lighted pipe in the barn after milking the cows. Despite this painful experience, they resolved to rebuild the barn.

Within a year, a new barn, painted red, stood near the site of the original barn. This barn was a one story structure that had an addition on the rear to house cattle.

In their early years at the farm they had a large gray horse and a carriage to provide transportation. With both the horse and carriage gone, they decided my grandfather would learn to drive a car, which they would buy and keep in the new barn. It was in the fall of 1933 when the plan to finally buy a car was taking place. It was something they looked forward to with much anticipation, and wanted to share with the entire family. Late on a Saturday afternoon, when the air was still warm and the smoke and scent of burning leaves hung over the neighborhood, my father was shaving at the kitchen sink, alongside the open kitchen door. It was close to supper time. Something caught his eye; he moved into the doorway for a better look and shouted to my mother, "Mary, the new barn is on fire!" It had happened again, just about eighteen months after losing the first barn in the same way. Not much was saved this time. Even the favorite cow of the family, Blacky, did not survive the blaze. The emotional impact on my grandparents was great, and the hopes of owning and driving a car rested in the ashes of the new red barn. Though they continued to farm on a smaller scale, this time they did not replace the barn.

Perhaps it was their deep religious faith that sustained my grandparents during times of adversity. Maybe it was an inherited trait, a character strength, or a special kind of courage. It may have been all these things blended together, a combination of grace, strength and faith; the same qualities that sustained them in their move from their native land to a new world. They might bend, weep and be grieved by the circumstances of life, but they would not allow defeat. Their tenacity of spirit would not permit that. And if they kept score, they surely knew that their gains far exceeded their losses, especially when we count the love they gave and received.

CHAPTER **10**

A Winter of Dark Mornings
◆◆◆

For reasons that are not quite clear, it seems there was a strong correlation between being a miner and drinking alcohol. It may have been the stress associated with that highly dangerous occupation. Perhaps it was a combination of circumstances: mining, trying to establish roots in a new world, raising a family and fighting the emotional effects of the prolonged economic depression. Maybe it was simply a socializing habit that got out of hand and was really more of an individual problem than was apparent at the time. Whatever it was, drinking seemed to be a natural part of the mining culture, an atmosphere in which strong men worked hard, played hard and, when time allowed, enjoyed socializing to the fullest. For many it was as natural as eating or breathing; it made the rough edges of life a bit smoother and added a certain pleasure to personal interactions. It was a way of entertaining, relaxing and celebrating the milestones in life with friends. It had a place in their society, a place that many could keep in perspective and suffer no harm. For some it became a burden that affected the quality of their lives and that of others.

My father was not immune to the customs of the time, and there is some indication he may have joined with his co-workers in the socializing and drinking rituals in his late teens. One of the reasons my mother's parents were reluctant to approve of the proposed marriage between my mother and father was the rumor that he occasionally drank too much. However, once the marriage took place, my father got along very well with my grandparents, even spending three years living in their home. It appears his tendency to drink started to become a problem in the early 1930s, perhaps about twelve years after my parents' marriage. The serious episodes usually took place every two weeks, on pay days. When he didn't arrive home at the usual time on a pay day, my mother, feeling he must have stopped with friends at one or more taverns, became quite uneasy. In addition to being concerned about his safety, she worried that he might spend a large part of his paycheck before he got home. It had happened before.

Eventually, he would come home, often quite late and showing the effects of drinking. My mother invariably became quite distraught and tearful. That there would be a shortage of money in the household before the next pay day was a prime issue. An even larger issue was the possibility of his being injured while drinking; being unable to work would place his job in jeopardy. The discussions on the recurring drinking bouts would escalate into arguments about providing for family needs, sharing responsibility, taking care of the children, ruining his health and placing himself in danger while driving when he was in no condition to do so. Motivated by her concern for him and the entire family, she would attempt to fix the problem by using the only tools she had: persuasion, pleading, weeping and mostly love. Eventually, my father, wanting to sleep off the effects of the alcohol, would call an end to any further discussion. It always ended in the same way; he would tell my mother to "take your pups and get out of the house!"

Sometimes, my father allowed Pat to stay in the house with him, but most of the time Pat left with the rest of us. When the weather would allow it, my mother would take Pat, Ruth, and me to the end of our back yard where we would quietly wait under an apple tree until my father fell asleep. Normally, it was a relatively short time until he was in a deep sleep and we could go back inside. Being put out of the house during bad weather, however, created additional problems for my mother since we usually went to my grandparents' house when we could not stay outdoors. My mother seemed to prefer that to going to a neighbor's home or next door to the home of her sister, Annie. It was, apparently, easier for her to share the embarrassment with her parents than with others. While it must have given some comfort to my mother to have the close support of her parents, she was always reluctant to burden them with this serious personal problem. Once involved, they naturally tried to help in any way possible, often adding an emotional complication to the situation that my mother did not need.

It was always surprising how quickly the home situation returned to normal once my father recovered from a drinking binge. He and my mother reconciled quickly; he promising to conquer the habit that was bringing so much discord into the family and she anxiously seizing even the smallest hope that this time things would get much better. The greatest motivation for reconciliation was that they cared deeply for each other. My mother's sister, Antoinette, attributed their ability to heal the rifts between them to the fact that, "They were always lovers; no matter how bad things got, they could always make up." There was a certain joy to their making up that affected all of us. It was good to see my father being himself, my mother relaxed, and both of them happy. The atmosphere was once again pleasant and normal; my parents happily working together in and around our home and all of us enjoying the sunlight that followed the storm. There was a need to believe, especially for my mother, that the most recent episode was going to be the last. And when my father made his promises to overcome his drinking habit, there was no doubt that he was sincere. At the time, however, no one, including my parents, had any idea how little control my father had over the addiction that was affecting all of us.

Occasionally, when my father lost his battle to stay sober, he would not return home for two or three days at a time. It was never certain where he was, and this added another great element of concern to the situation. During Christmas week of 1936, after Christmas but before New Year's Eve, my father left on a drinking binge and stayed away from home for at least two days. Having him gone at that particular time of the year was especially difficult; it seemed to magnify our worries and contrasted sharply with the happy spirits within the home just a few days past. It turned out that on December 30 he was in Simpson and likely met with friends at one or more taverns. At some point in the early afternoon he decided to leave his car in Simpson and walk home, even though there was approximately one foot of snow on the ground. Instead of following the road to Whites Crossing and from there to our home, he chose to walk uphill through woods and field areas. Along the way the effects of the alcohol and the exertion of walking uphill through snow made him extremely tired. He decided to rest under a tree and fell asleep in the snow. He slept for over an hour and awoke severely chilled and wet. When he arrived home, it was evident that he was quite ill.

Relieved to have him home and recognizing the traumatic experience he had endured, my mother helped him to clean up and get into dry clothes. Early in the evening of December 30 he visited our family physician with my mother. Following some treatment, he returned home and retired early, intent on going to work the next day. While his illness made for a fitful sleep, he arose before six o'clock and started to dress for work. Getting dressed soon used up more energy than he had acquired over the night. Going into the kitchen, where my mother was fixing breakfast, he told her that he was not feeling well enough to work that day. Concerned about his job and the dire need for every day's pay, she protested. He then suggested, maybe as a way of making up, that they bake a cake for Gene's first birthday, which was on the following day. He also proposed that my mother visit her sister, Antoinette, later in the morning and invite her to bring her two young daughters over to our home to attend a small birthday party for Gene. Seeing that he really was not feeling well, liking his suggestion, and wanting to make things right between them once again, she agreed. He then offered to go to the basement to get the cake pans they would need for the birthday cake. Before too long, he started to walk up the stairs from the basement slowly and in great discomfort, without the cake pans. His illness was more serious than either of them realized.

My mother helped him to undress and put him in the bedroom Pat and I normally used. Being next to the kitchen and having only one window, it was warmer than my parents' bedroom. By seven o'clock, she went to the McDonald's home across the street to use their telephone to call our family physician. Dr. Kauffman was at our home within an hour and began treating my father immediately. Later, Dr. Oblazney, a relative of my grandfather, arrived at our home to assist Dr. Kauffman; the family wanted all the medical help they could get. Both doctors concurred in the diagnosis: lobar pneumonia.

Before nine-thirty the news of my father's illness spread to numerous family members and neighbors. Our house became crowded with people wanting to share their concern and support my parents. My father's brother, Joseph, arrived with two of his sisters. Babkee and Jadkee were there early, along with my aunts, Annie, Antoinette and Antoinette's husband, Stanley. Our neighbors, Mrs. Zukowski, Mrs. Falong, and the McDonald sisters, came to assist the family as best they could. Some of my older cousins who lived next door wandered in and out throughout the morning. The volume of people heightened the fear I was beginning to feel and added to the somber atmosphere that filled the house. Everyone, it seemed, wanted to stand in our sitting room so they could look into the adjoining bedroom where the doctors treated my father.

By ten forty-five my father lay in bed, propped up by pillows piled behind him to ease his labored breathing. He requested a cigarette and the doctors, hoping it might help him relax, agreed. An older cousin of mine lit the cigarette and held it to his lips, but he lacked the strength to puff it. The soft weeping that had gone on most of the morning among those who waited and watched became more audible. Being small in height and weight, I found it increasingly difficult to see my father; the grown-ups had unknowingly maneuvered me into the far corner of the sitting room. I had to peer left or right around the adults to catch a glimpse of my father. His face, showing the effects of the fever, pain and great distress, was gray and damp. He looked worn and exhausted. His condition frightened my mother to the verge of hysteria. Alternately, she would encourage my father, holding his hand or touching his face, then plead with the doctors to do more to ease his pain and make him feel better. Lacking any other means of helping him, my mother seemed resolved to make him well through the strength of her will and desire.

Someone, perhaps a priest called to our home, suggested that we all join in a recitation of the Rosary, a powerful prayer for divine assistance in the crisis. As the praying started, some knelt on the floor while others prayed where they stood. I was in the corner, near the door to the pantry and close to the day bed against the outside wall. I knelt at the end of the day bed and prayed as earnestly and emphatically as I could, all the while deeply regretting that I had not been a better student of religion so that my prayers might have more worth. The entire gathering praying with such sincerity made me feel somewhat better. God, I thought, will surely hear the voices of so many seeking the same thing. I was wrong. For whatever reasons, our prayers didn't work. Nothing worked. Shortly before noon, my father died. It was Thursday, December 31, 1936. He was thirty-seven.

The sudden, unexpected death of my father was bewildering and seemed unreal. It had come too swiftly, a stunning end to what initially appeared to be nothing more than a serious cold. His death seemed to be unjustified. None of us were ready to deal with a sudden emotional shock of that magnitude, and my first reaction was to disbelieve what had taken place. Perhaps it was a child's way of dealing with an event too difficult to accept, but I felt that a terrible mistake had occurred, one that had to be fixed quickly. Slowly and unwillingly, as preparations began for his funeral, I began to realize that this tragedy was not fixable.

The next day a newspaper article on my father's death appeared in *The Scranton Tribune*. The writer obviously knew him well. After describing the short duration of his illness and the shock that his sudden death brought to the community, the writer outlined my father's work history and his affiliation with Saint Rose Church and the Holy Name Society. Then he expressed his own thoughts and that of others when he wrote, "He was a young man of most cordial disposition who enjoyed a host of acquaintances and friends, and his death will be deeply mourned."

For our family the public mourning followed the custom of that time: a three-day viewing, more commonly known then as a wake, took place at our home. A large arrangement of flowers in a basket hung to the right of our front door. The flowers served as a symbol to those passing by that someone within the household had died and a wake was being held. Family and friends came to our home throughout each day and evening to express sympathy, visit, and console. Much of the community banded together, as it had for other wakes, to assist the family in any way it could and offer as much comfort as possible. They also brought food and drinks of all types to feed the family as well as those who traveled a long distance to attend the wake or funeral. The term "wake" simply meant that some of the mourners would remain awake throughout the night, much like an honor guard, for the one who had died. For them the long nights passed more easily because of the food and drinks available.

My father lay in state in our parlor, to the left of the room as mourners entered through the front door. Flowers sent by family and friends as an expression of sympathy were all around him, and lamps providing indirect lighting softly illuminated the area. Many of those who did not send flowers brought a mass card from a church. The cards meant they had arranged with a priest for the celebration of a mass for the soul of my father. As people entered the house, they placed the mass cards in a tray near the casket; since this was a very religious community, the tray soon overflowed. Folding chairs crowded the parlor and sitting room, allowing only a pathway from the front door to the kitchen. On each evening of the three-day wake, many people found only standing room in our home due to the number of visitors calling.

For my mother, the entry of each mourner into our home would trigger a new wave of anguished weeping, an emotional response that quickly affected everyone present. During periods when no new visitors were entering the house, the atmosphere was a bit calmer. The women tended to take chairs next to each other in our sitting room while the men gathered in our kitchen to talk, exchange memories of my father, and smoke. The ladies would alternately weep softly, talk about their families, smile at a story they just heard and then return to mourning as my mother tearfully greeted another visitor. The mixture of normal exchanges between friends and the periodic grieving was confusing to me; I did not understand at the time that, even as we mourn, life continues. For me the entire period of the wake was chaotic and scary; it seemed unreal, like a nightmare that returned every morning when I awoke.

At nine-thirty in the morning on Monday, January 4, 1937, we gathered at Saint Rose Church for the celebration of a requiem mass for my father. The large number of people attending the service was impressive; it seemed they had come not only to mourn but to celebrate his life as well. Following the mass a caravan of cars traveled to Our Mother of Sorrows Cemetery, located on a large hill about two miles outside of Carbondale, for the burial. The single plot at the western edge of the cemetery cost $60.00, which my mother had to borrow from her parents. The solemn graveside service took place in bitter cold, the wind blowing fiercely across the frozen landscape. We stayed cold for a very long time.

The positive aspects of a wake include the company and close support that is available, at least until the funeral takes place. When the care-givers returned to their families the stillness of our home magnified the void within our lives and brought into sharp focus the reality that we would be a family without a father. Perhaps it is the abruptness with which reality arrives that allows the emotionally wounded to begin finding the strength to survive in the world, reorganize their lives, and move on. It would be a slow and confusing process, however, because shock and anguish diminish at such a slow pace.

As my mother worried about our future and struggled to cope with the chaos that had come into our lives, we had the obligation to attend masses held for my father at Saint Rose Church. These were the spiritual gifts people had brought to his wake. There was no question about our being there since the masses were a significant religious ritual for the deceased, and we wanted to be at every one we could possibly attend. Most of them were at six o'clock in the morning, two or three times a week. At the time I thought the reason they were so early was that the last person to die automatically got the earliest mass time. Our 1931 Chevrolet was in the garage, but my mother did not drive and

Pat was not old enough for a driver's license. That meant we had to walk to Saint Rose, a distance of one and a half miles. The early morning cold and snow always made it seem much longer.

My mother woke us about five o'clock, when the first light of morning was still a long way off. We took turns at the single sink in the kitchen to clear the sleep from our faces, comb our hair, and brush our teeth. As I waited my turn I always looked out of a front window, toward the street light near the McDonald home, to check the weather. Seeing the blowing, drifting snow that covered the road helped me to gauge what the walk to church would be like. We did not have breakfast before we left because of the necessity to fast before receiving communion. Pulling on our boots, getting into our warmest jackets, wool hats and gloves, we left the house while our adopted sister Mary stayed behind with Gene. The darkness seemed to add an extra level of sharpness to the first few gulps of frigid air. We walked on the road for the first quarter mile before we got to the point where there were sidewalks. Most often, snow covered the sidewalks, so we continued to walk on the road in the tracks left by milk trucks that had come through an hour earlier making home deliveries. The four of us walked in silence, our gloved hands stuffed in our pockets as we leaned into the wind blowing into our faces. Trudging along, we moved from one street light to another, fading in and out of darkness until we reached the church.

The masses, usually held in the lower level of Saint Rose Church, attracted a small number of people at that hour of the morning. Along with our family of four, about three dozen people would be present, many of whom came to that early service on a regular basis. Generally, the service was not very long, but when we left the church I always felt we had done something good for our father and for ourselves as well. By the time we finished the long, uphill walk to our home, the darkness would begin to give way to the first faint light of dawn. The house would be warmer because both the furnace and the kitchen stove had been stoked. Our breakfast was often toast made over the hot coals, smeared with margarine and dipped in catsup. Hot coffee did a lot to get rid of the chill. Before eight o'clock we were on our way to school.

As we grew older and reached certain milestones in life I tended to wonder what my father's reaction might have been to each significant event. He had gone too soon, before we had passed through our formative years. When important milestones occurred, the sense of regret that he was not present to share our triumphs and joys had a double edge to it. I was never sure which was the greater disappointment; that he missed those good things or that we missed having him with us to share them. More than a few decades would pass before I gained a more realistic acceptance of the situation and my feelings of regret became less poignant. Eventually, my understanding of what had taken place evolved to a different level; I came to realize that those who leave too soon alter and form our lives to the same extent as those who remain with us.

CHAPTER 11

Red Racer Wagon

◆◆◆

Spring of 1937 brought with it a welcome relief from the gloom of that particular winter and added a small measure of warmth and brightness to our lives. We were a long way from adjusting to the fact that we were a family without a father; everything in and about our home, especially the memories, reminded us of the magnitude of our loss. But in ways that were not apparent at the time, we began to accept the fact that our new condition was not going to change; the family now had one parent and four children, a circumstance that caused considerable apprehension but at the same time drew us closer together. Losing the father of our family seemed to make each of those remaining a more valued member of our household. For me, it was as if I were seeing each member of the family in a new light, finding them all more important than they had ever been.

For my mother the adjustment was much more difficult. Not only had she lost a husband and her closest friend, but she also suddenly had thrust upon her the sole responsibility for a home and four children, a burden that was as frightening as it was overwhelming. The need to find a source of income became more urgent with each passing month, not only for the basic necessities of living, but to avoid losing the home through default on mortgage payments. Each time she considered working outside the home, the issue of Gene's care became a matter of great concern since he was just a year old and a nursing baby. After exploring numerous options with her parents and sisters, she reached the conclusion she would have to earn a living by working at home. She decided to put to use her locally recognized talent for baking bread, pies, cakes and a variety of other fine-tasting foods. A small bakery operating out of the home would become the chief source of family income. This decision took an exceptional amount of courage since she had never before attempted a venture of this magnitude or importance. At stake was the welfare of her family and the retention of her home. Clearly understanding the risks involved, she began the small business intensely determined to make it succeed.

Realizing that the coal stove in our small kitchen could handle only a modest amount of baking, she had a second stove installed in our basement. Essentially, this provided two baking centers, the larger one being in the basement. We collected spare bread pans, cake pans, cookie sheets and pie dishes from family and neighbors and bought others. A large supply of flour, sugar, spices and condiments of all types filled our pantries. Word of her proposed business filtered throughout the area, and numerous families expressed interest in our bakery. Although small in number, there were customers for the new business, many of whom were friends and relatives. The plan was fairly simple; my mother, with Ruth's assistance, would do the baking and Pat and I would make the deliveries. With all preparations made and her fears held tightly in check, my mother was ready to put the bakery into operation. All we needed was some way to deliver the baked goods through Whites Crossing, parts of Simpson and the upper end of Canaan Street.

I am not sure where it came from, but a wagon showed up at our house at about the time we were ready to start the small bakery. It was no ordinary vehicle, but a Red Racer wagon, a strong, durable, well-designed and carefully built wagon. Made of nicely finished oak wood and coated with varnish, it was impressive. The large, rectangular box of the wagon was about five inches deep and equipped with metal brackets on all four sides. Staked sides, consisting of three evenly spaced oak slats mounted on sturdy oak stakes, came with the wagon. The staked sides, when placed into the brackets, greatly increased the wagon's capacity. They also allowed us to create shelves by inserting thin boards from one side of the wagon to the other. In this way we could carry a variety of baked goods without any of them being crushed. Along with a long steering and pulling handle, the wagon had unusual wheels. They had red wooden spokes held in place by a steel band that served as a kind of "tire," a rather noisy tire. Bright red letters on each side of the box announced that this was a Red Racer, the ultimate wagon. It was a very handsome wagon, the likes of which we had never seen before.

On weekdays my mother would arise early in the morning to start the bread dough since getting it ready for the oven was a time-consuming process. As the bread was rising and being kneaded periodically, she prepared the cakes and pies we hoped to sell that day. By the time we got home from school, everything was just about ready for delivery. Ruth helped my mother to place the still-warm bread in paper bags and carefully cover the cakes and pies with waxed paper. Pat and I would arrange the baked goods in the wagon in a way that made the best use of all the space. Once we were ready, we headed for the first homes along the road to Whites Crossing. Until we established a regular customer base, we went door to door selling our baked goods, each of us going to different houses to cover as much territory as possible. As we sold loaves of bread or other items, we placed the money we collected in a canvas bag. Early on, some customers wanted to buy on credit, agreeing to pay us every two weeks. I was almost ten but not much of a bookkeeper, so Pat kept a record of the credit purchases. My mother's bread was in big demand, and when we sold the last loaf on the wagon, we hurried home to get more.

    The busiest day by far was always Saturday. In addition to bread, more people wanted to buy sweet-tasting baked goods for the weekend. While certain preparations took place the night before, the volume of work to be done to meet our delivery schedule required my mother and Ruth to begin work early in the morning. Though she was only eleven when the bakery business began, Ruth was my mother's chief baking assistant and the two worked side by side throughout long Saturday mornings turning out bread and a variety of pastries, and cleaning an endless array of pots, pans and dishes. My mother, in teaching Ruth to spread icing on cakes and cupcakes and do a bit of decorating, discovered that Ruth was not quite tall enough to do the job easily and well. Her solution was to get a wooden soda case and turn it upside down to make a five-inch platform. It worked so well it became an essential kitchen tool for Ruth.

    While the baking was in progress, Pat and I would haul coal for the stoves, remove the ashes, fetch and carry things for my mother and Ruth, and help to place the bread in bags. Occasionally, we would sample the sweets; our rationale was that we should be able to describe to our customers how good they were. Everything was always very good, and the variety of baked goods was extensive. Although the offerings changed almost daily, over a period of a month we sold donuts, cakes, pies, hot cross buns, cinnamon rolls, cupcakes and some Polish delicacies. One, called *kajzerki*, resembled a diamond-shaped croissant filled with a sweetened mixture of cottage cheese and spices. It seemed to be a favorite of many customers. Another popular item was a cupcake called a "lafayette." Dipped in a liquid jelly and then heavily coated with grated coconut, the cupcakes looked as good as they tasted. They sold so fast that the customers at the end of our last route rarely got to buy them. The breads were a standard that always sold well, especially my mother's mashed potato bread and rolls.

By ten o'clock Saturday morning Pat and I would be on our way with the first wagon load of bakery items. Our customers learned to expect us and, along with buying one or two loaves of bread, they always asked about pastries or came to the wagon to look them over. When they came to look, they usually bought some type of pastry. We collected money as we sold, including some from customers who had previously bought on credit. As the wagon emptied, we returned home for a new load and headed out to another route. The routine continued year round because the narrow, steel-banded wheels made it fairly easy to pull the wagon through the snow and it could handle a substantial load of baked goods. However, going into Simpson during the summer months could be grueling due to the effort required to pull the wagon uphill in the heat on the return home.

Many times Pat and I would finish our routes by four o'clock Saturday afternoon, most often with everything sold out. My mother would give each of us fifteen cents and allow us to go to Carbondale to see a movie at the Majestic Theater, a place that featured cowboy movies. We would remove the staked sides from our Red Racer wagon since it would be our transportation into town. Canaan Street consisted of two successive hills, with the first one starting about a quarter mile from our home. The first part was fairly steep while the second was a challenge, going down or coming up. At the time the paving for the entire street was oversized bricks. When we got to the top of the first hill, we'd jump in the wagon, with Pat driving. Our riding style was always the same; it would be full speed all the way to stay with the traffic flow. Steel-rimmed wheels racing over the uneven brick road made for a bone-jarring ride accompanied by an ungodly amount of noise. People walking on the sidewalks or working in their yards would stop to watch us go by. And drivers gave us room, a lot of room. It was a spectacular ride.

When we got to town we pulled our wagon to the Anthracite Hotel, where Mary, our "adopted" sister and family member, worked as a waitress. She arranged for us to store our wagon in a shed behind the hotel while we were at the movies. We went see to Tom Mix, Johnny Mack Brown, Tim McCoy, a young Gene Autry and Roy Rogers, plus one of the chapters. There were always chapters. Chapters were movie serials, each about twenty minutes in length and continuing for about ten weeks. Each chapter ended with the hero in a serious dilemma, a situation where escape appeared impossible. That tended to keep the crowd coming back to see how the hero got away. They were a lot of fun. Leaving the theater, we would return to the Anthracite Hotel where Mary would treat us to a dessert and drink before we walked back home pulling our wagon. It was a good way to end a long day.

Within six months of starting the bakery it was obvious to my mother that it was going to be a success. We were meeting living expenses, including the mortgage and other bills, and saving small amounts. We were making it; not by much, perhaps, but enough to keep the family going. The relief my mother felt was probably greater than the pleasure that came from seeing this high risk venture succeed. There were no big celebrations, however, since we all realized that we still had a long way to go. Instead, we simply enjoyed the sense of satisfaction that came from the modest success of the business that was so important to us. Much of the satisfaction came from the fact that we were more than a family with a small bakery; we were a family team working as best we could for each other, with our mother providing the talent, strength and determination to make it succeed.

Our bakery business lasted about two years, from the spring of 1937 until April, 1939. It ended when our mother, overworked and exhausted for a long time, became ill with pneumonia. While Pat, Ruth and I played strong, supporting roles in the operation of the business, our mother was the force that made it work. There was no one to take her place, even for a little while, and we were in school, too young and inexperienced to do the things that she could do so well. Within a few weeks of her illness it became clear the bakery business would close. For us the abrupt ending was a shock. We were into a routine and felt comfortable with the work. The fact that people liked what we sold and we were contributing to the family's livelihood gave us a sense of accomplishment and pride, even though it kept us busy six days a week. Something good came to a stop when we least expected it. Again, family income became a major concern. Our mother realized, however, that even if she recovered quickly, the workload was too heavy and the pace too constant to keep the business operating for an extended period of time. As it turned out, it was more than a month before she began to feel a bit better.

As the news spread regarding my mother's illness and the close of the bakery, our customers were genuinely saddened. They knew the importance of the small business to our family, and they had come to depend on the delivery of quality baked goods to their homes.

One of the issues associated with the closing of the bakery was the settlement of accounts and the recovery of amounts owed from those who bought baked goods on credit. Pat made most of the collection contacts and, with some exceptions, did very well. Most honored their obligation to clear their accounts, but there was a small number who, for reasons unknown to us, never paid. While the passage of time has lessened the keen disappointment we felt when we realized some were not going to pay their debts, Pat can still recite their names.

There is one small matter related to our bakery business for which we have not found an explanation, and that concerns the Red Racer wagon. As we began to establish the bakery, the lack of money was critical, so it is unlikely our mother bought the wagon. If someone gave or loaned it to us, there is no recollection of that, not even by older relatives who lived close by and had a strong personal interest in every aspect of the new business. A clear explanation was never uncovered for the timely appearance of the wagon at the time the bakery was founded or its sudden disappearance when the small enterprise ended. The simple fact is, we don't know where the Red Racer wagon came from, or what became of it after the bakery closed.

CHAPTER 12

Blue Shirts and Gray Knickers

◆◆◆

My mother, recovering slowly from pneumonia, worried as the modest amount of money she was able to save from the bakery business steadily decreased. Even if her health had allowed her to work, jobs in the area were scarce; it would be a few more years before the Great Depression lost its grip on the country. My grandparents always helped the family with food from their farm, and when they could afford it, they gave her a few spare dollars. Such assistance was not a long-term solution, however, and my mother had great difficulty accepting their help since Jadkee was in his ninth year of retirement, a retirement that did not bring with it a pension of any amount. For him Social Security was also nonexistent since he had retired before it became law. The bleak outlook was especially difficult since it contrasted so sharply with the recent success of our bakery and the good feelings that came from knowing we were able to take care of ourselves.

During the Depression years, the state and federal governments developed numerous relief programs to aid the unemployed and those whose income was not sufficient to support a family. For many households, having at least one person employed did not ensure prosperity. Often, the earnings were so meager that most families were just a few steps above the poverty threshold. But, since it was a common standard, it tended to put everyone on the same level. Applying for relief, however, meant the family had slipped below the standard, a situation most families wanted to avoid. As a community, the families were poor but proud. Still, lacking other alternatives, my mother reluctantly decided she would have to apply for state aid until she could find another way to support the family.

The program for which she qualified, Mothers' Assistance, focused on helping widows with children. When we applied for aid, our home became a kind of collateral to ensure the state would one day be reimbursed for the assistance it provided. Essentially, it was a lien against the property, a legality that made certain the state would receive its rightful share should the house be sold. My mother qualified easily for assistance and the monthly checks began to arrive. Each one was a reminder of the family's poor financial situation and the growing debt that, at some point in the future, must be paid. She became increasingly determined to limit state assistance by returning to work as soon as possible. Along with the checks, the state distributed food in bulk quantities every month. Among the foods provided were flour, sugar, beans, powdered milk, corn meal, potatoes and a yellow-colored lard that passed for margarine. Also distributed were slabs of bacon, cheese and, occasionally, meat. The Armory located on Eighth Avenue in Carbondale was the distribution point for much of the bulk and canned food. The dairy products and meat, for reasons that are not clear, came from a distribution center in Simpson that was next to Banko's small theater.

Picking up the food each month was a chore that Pat and I shared. Usually, he went to Simpson while I went to Carbondale and, by itself, it was not a difficult task. For me the hard part came with my being excused from class at the Robert Morris School once every month about two-thirty in the afternoon. Miss Mary

McDonald was my teacher at the time as well as the school principal. In addition, she and her family lived across the street from our home and were friends as well as neighbors. She was a fine, compassionate lady, deeply concerned about the welfare of my mother and her family. As a result, she wanted to be certain I never missed going for our food allotment. I would have preferred to leave quietly and unnoticed, but that never happened. Miss McDonald would begin glancing at the clock in the school room at about two-fifteen, getting ready to excuse me, and since I was the only one in the room scheduled to leave to pick up welfare food, it was acutely embarrassing. I could feel my face getting flushed and a fine sweat break out on my upper lip as the clock moved closer to two-thirty. When she finally said, "It is time for you to go, Donald," I hurried out of the classroom as fast as I could and ran home feeling frustrated and resentful. Later, I would realize how foolish my response was at the time. The only reaction I ever sensed from my classmates was quiet acceptance. Perhaps it was because they realized that someday they might be joining me on the trip to Carbondale.

While getting food from the Mothers' Assistance program created a small problem for me, the clothing provided under the program was a much greater issue. The clothes Pat and I got were not at all stylish or fancy, but they were new, well-made and sturdy. Obviously made by the thousands under a contract with the state or federal government, the shirts came in one color, a light blue. Made to be work shirts, they had long sleeves, a pocket on the left front and white buttons. The material appeared to be a light denim. Like the shirts, the knickers came in one color, medium gray. Well made from a light, canvas-type cloth, they were quite rugged. Being knickers, the pant legs came down to a point just below the knee where they buttoned to keep them snug over long stockings that came to the same point. Since he was four years older and perhaps more style conscious, Pat would not wear those clothes to school. He would wear the shirts while at home, but I am not sure he ever wore the knickers. The clothes that Ruth got seemed to come in greater variety; this made them less easily identified with the welfare program. The same was true of the outer wear we received, especially the winter coats. I don't recall that any clothes were available for my mother under the program.

I wore my blue shirts and gray knickers to school with great reluctance. I was old enough to realize that this was the uniform of the poor, the distinctive colors advertising to the world that our family needed help to survive. That there were other boys in school wearing the same uniform did not do much to ease my discomfort. When I wore those clothes to school the first few times, I watched defensively for any reaction. There was none. There seemed to be an understanding among the students, even though we were all quite young, that these were difficult times and we did what was necessary to get by. It occurred to many, I think, they might soon be wearing the blue and gray themselves. One event took place in school that helped convince me that perhaps the clothes really didn't matter that much; on February fourteenth I got many valentines, a few of which I have never forgotten.

Shortly after the bakery closed, Pat managed to secure a large newspaper delivery route from *The Scranton Tribune*, a morning newspaper. It consisted of our immediate neighborhood, Whites Crossing, Number Four Road to a point well beyond the school, Number Seven Road just opposite the school, and that part of Simpson that bordered Whites Crossing. The large size and scattered nature of the route required both of us to make deliveries before school started. Generally, we divided the routes between the hilly area and the relatively flat area, and we switched routes from time to time. To speed his deliveries, Pat bought an old bike for fifty cents at the Salvation Army. It didn't have any tires and the brakes were all but nonexistent. Pat made his own tires by cutting pieces of garden hose and half-inch steel cables to fit precisely around each wheel. He threaded the cable through each piece of hose, fitted it to the wheel and secured it in place around the rim with wire. It wasn't fancy and the ride was a bit bumpy, but it worked quite well. Stopping was a challenge, one that involved a lot of foot work.

During the winter newspaper deliveries were made while it was still dark, a fact that caused me to take along a flashlight for the sense of security it provided. I'm not sure why I felt concerned, but I liked the idea of seeing what might be coming toward me. As it turned out, when the first opportunity came to use it, I didn't turn it on. I was part way up Number Four Road, just above Rushen's store, passing the two Plevyak family homes on opposite sides of the road. Moving along the snow-covered road and not paying attention, I came to a sudden stop in front of a large man in dark clothing. He had a cigarette in his mouth and was carrying a lunch pail, obviously on his way to work. He grunted something I did not understand but I assumed meant he wanted a newspaper. I handed one to him and he gave me three cents, the cost of the paper. He grunted again and headed downhill while I continued going up, relieved that the encounter had been so normal. Over the next few months I continued to meet him at some point on the hill. We'd stop, he'd hand me three cents and I'd give him a paper. He would mumble a single word, one I never understood, and then move on. After a while I did not meet him anymore. I never knew who he was or where he was going. Most likely, he switched to a different work shift, but since we kept the paper routes for about two years, I always thought I would see him again. While we did not know each other and never really conversed, we established a brief rapport, resulting, perhaps, from the fact that two people of vastly different ages were out in the early morning dark, each earning a living.

While Pat and I continued with the paper route, our mother's health improved and she found some work cleaning houses for a few reasonably affluent families on lower Canaan Street. The work was hard, low paying and periodic, but it did supplement the relief checks while she searched for better paying, full-time employment. At home Ruth remained her chief assistant in all aspects of maintaining a household, with Gene's care being a priority. At the same time, her cooking and baking skills flourished under my mother's guidance. Though we were getting by, our mother worried continually about not having a job that could support the family and permit her to discontinue the Mothers' Assistance program. The ever-increasing size of the lien against our home greatly concerned her. While she was happy to have aid during a difficult period, having to accept it made her feel quite uncomfortable. It became increasingly apparent that, to change the unhappy circumstances, she would have to widen the employment circle to include areas beyond Simpson and Carbondale.

At about that time more and more people from the Whites Crossing and Simpson communities were taking jobs at Darlington Fabrics, a textile manufacturer in Newton, New Jersey. Although Newton was only seventy miles southeast of Whites Crossing, jobs at Darlington were plentiful and the pay was good. Car pools of workers would leave Whites Crossing and Simpson to travel to Newton on Sunday evenings. They stayed with families in Newton who provided room and board throughout the work week and then traveled back to their homes after completing work on Friday. While not an ideal situation, the jobs were a salvation for the many who would otherwise not be working. My mother's decision to join the group working in Newton did not come easily; only the constant assurance of her parents and her sisters that they would look in on us frequently gave her the courage to go. Her decision emphasized how desperate her situation was and her determination to make things better for all of us. She was a remarkably kind and sensitive lady, one who could be a bit shy, but in matters pertaining to the welfare of her family she was absolutely fearless, even when scared to death.

In all, the family was under the Mothers' Assistance program for about eight months, and all welfare ended when my mother took a job at Darlington Fabrics. Although there were many apprehensions about having our mother gone for most of the week, we tended to think of the job as a new opportunity for the entire family. In a sense, it was a bit like the bakery business with each of us having some responsibility in making the arrangement a success. In a place that at the time seemed very far away, she would do the work essential to support the family while we would take care of the house and each other. Like the bakery, it would turn out to be an achievement, but one that came with a price. We missed her for all the reasons children living alone would miss a parent, and while some called it a character building experience, we became a lot older than we should have been at that age.

CHAPTER **13**

Lady of the House
━━━━━━━━ ◆◆◆ ━━━━━━━━

Shortly after my father died, relatives came to our garage, jacked up the 1931 Chevrolet at all four wheels, and placed it on blocks. Having the wheels raised off the floor, they reasoned, would keep the tires from rotting until the family drove the car again. My mother had little interest in driving while my father was alive, partly because it seemed to be a male responsibility then and because her many aptitudes did not include working with mechanical things. Uncomfortable with the idea of driving, she avoided applying for a learner's permit and taking lessons for almost two years after the death of my father. As it became more apparent that she might have to take employment at a company that was not within walking distance, she found the fortitude to begin driving. When the job opportunity came at Darlington Fabrics, she was ready to try some long distance traveling.

She began her employment near the end of 1939 and, being assigned to the night shift, she decided to drive to Newton on her own instead of commuting with others. This gave her a little more flexibility in leaving home on Monday about noon and returning home promptly after her shift ended at eleven o'clock on Friday evenings. The driving time to Newton was about two hours, but it was a trip my mother dreaded. Part of her concern was due to her inexperience in driving and trying to follow route signs, especially at night. A much greater concern was the passage on Route Six through the wilds of Pike County. This stretch of sparsely settled forests extended for about twenty-five miles, with few occupied cabins or homes and no gas stations. Our Chevrolet had a tendency to break a rear axle without warning, and the thought of being stranded at night in Pike County made each trip an anxiety-filled adventure. Somehow, she always found the courage to face her fears and complete the trip.

The week prior to her leaving for Newton for the first time was one of great preparation. In addition to packing the things she would take to the boarding house, she baked bread, rolls, and cake and gave us detailed instructions on what we were to do and not do. Recognizing the seriousness of this discussion, we sat quietly on the day bed in our sitting room and listened attentively while my mother reviewed her list. Pat was sixteen, Ruth was thirteen, I was twelve, and Gene was three. Keeping the fires going and removing the ashes from stove and furnace were important items. Taking care of Gene and ensuring he was always out of harm's way was her chief concern. Immediately calling on Babkee or our Aunt Annie if problems arose was essential. As with most mothers facing a similar situation, she fretted and worried and tried to cover every possible contingency. For Pat, Ruth and me, the thought of living by ourselves and caring for a very young Gene was more than a bit serious, so we asked many "what if" questions and somberly thought about the weeks ahead. We understood why she had to go to Newton, but that did nothing to alleviate the feeling of loss, even before she left for the first time. We had become a team and she was the leader, a comforting presence in our home, one we were not quite ready to do without. But when the time came, we stood on the front porch smiling and waving as she drove away.

My mother's last instruction before she left was that Ruth would be in charge, the lady of the house. In giving Ruth that responsibility it was clear that my mother recognized that Ruth had become a smaller and younger version of herself and had learned her lessons well. Although lacking the experience that comes with repetition and age, she knew the basics of operating a household, including cooking. Most of all, it seems my mother sensed that Ruth would take really good care of Gene since she had all the instincts of a young, dependable mother. In retrospect, that was an extraordinary amount of responsibility to place on a girl who was not quite fourteen, but few choices existed since our adopted sister, Mary, married about five months earlier, was living with her new husband in the small town of Mayfield. While most of the time Pat and I did our assignments and the cooperation among the three of us was very good, Ruth had the added burden of our constant teasing about the quality of her cooking. Actually, it was fine, but it did present an opportunity for some fun while we sat around the kitchen table eating.

Walking into the house, we could easily tell when Ruth was making one of our favorite foods. The smell of onions being sauteed and sausage frying meant we were having long bologna. This was a sausage that looked like minced ham, but had a stronger, more distinct flavor. It was about three inches in diameter and, if we bought one whole sausage, it was about fifteen inches in length. Ruth would cut quarter-inch slices from the sausage and slowly fry them in a skillet until golden brown. We'd place the fried slices on homemade bread, cover them with sauteed onions, smear on some mustard and create the world's finest sandwich. The sandwich, accompanied by a side dish of hash brown potatoes, made a great-tasting meal. She usually made some dessert, which did not last very long. For a special treat she would occasionally make a dark, creamy fudge that contained bits of marshmallow and nuts. Spreading the mixture over a cookie sheet, she kept it in the coolest place in the house; on the concrete stairs leading from the basement to the outside. If we could have afforded an ice box for our kitchen, it would have saved many trips to our basement to sample the fudge.

When it came to taking care of Gene, there was no question that Ruth did much more than either Pat or I. During the week she dressed, fed, and bathed him, scheduled his naps and put him to bed each night at a regular hour. On weekends my mother did most of those things to give Ruth some relief. It also gave her the time she needed to spend with her baby before she returned to Newton. Pat and I helped with Gene as best we could, but our main contribution was in taking him outdoors, many times when we were playing games. We would often take him to a field between our home and Whites Crossing where we played ball. We'd place him under a shade tree to keep him out of the sun, and just about every player there took turns keeping him amused while the game progressed. He seemed to like everything we did to amuse him, even when some of the adventures were a bit risky. Sometimes we would take him out in his carriage and decide to give him a ride down the small hill at the back of our home. While one of us pushed the carriage to the top of the hill, the other waited at the bottom. Then, with the carriage pointed downhill, a hard push got it off to a fast start. It rolled down at a good speed with Gene loudly expressing his pleasure with the ride. The person at the foot of the hill had the job of stopping the carriage before it hit the house. There were many who disapproved of our little game although Pat, Gene and I thought it was great fun.

The wedding of our sister, Mary, took place in mid-1939, and my mother hosted a very pleasant reception at our home. Stanley Naumovitz, a young miner from the town of Mayfield, had courted Mary for almost two years. We took a liking to Stanley from the first time he called on Mary at our home. He was dark-haired, low-keyed and always very friendly, a relaxed, gentle young man. Every time he came to our home to visit Mary, we could be certain he would have chewing gum for us. One Christmas he gave each of us fifty cents, a generous amount back then. We liked the idea of Mary and Stanley being married; they seemed to be two perfectly matched people who had the good luck to find each other. It did seem strange, however, that Mary was leaving. She had been with us a long time, sharing in all aspects of our family life, the victories as well as the defeats. Her leaving at age twenty-two made me realize that eventually there would be a time for each of us to go, and Mary was first simply because she was the oldest. Family, neighbors and friends turned out for the wedding, and the celebration at our home was warm and special, the way it ought to be for a sister.

Pat graduated from Fell Township High School in 1941; shortly after, he joined the large number of friends and relatives from Whites Crossing and Simpson who worked at Darlington Fabrics in New Jersey. My mother, during the work week, stayed in a rooming house in Newton. Located in a nice residential area, the rooms were large and well cared for and the immigrant German owners were pleasant and accommodating. As a result, it pleased her when she arranged for Pat to stay at the same place. Pat's assignment to the day shift prompted my mother to let him drive the Chevrolet between Newton and Whites Crossing while she commuted with those from the area who began working the night shift hours with her. She had never felt even moderately comfortable driving to and from Newton alone, and the opportunity to be a passenger in a friend's car eliminated a very stressful activity. For Pat, who got his driver's license in 1940, the arrangement suited him perfectly because of a special interest in his life: her name was Helen Erzin. Pat was involved in some serious courting, one that did not allow for any weekends apart.

We first met Helen when Pat drove her to our home one weekend in the Chevrolet. He came up the driveway and parked the car near the back door and brought her into the kitchen. She was a very petite, slim young lady with large, expressive eyes and a radiant smile. Very well dressed with her hair carefully arranged to highlight her face, she obviously hoped to make a good first impression. She was highly successful. Pat had never before brought a girl home to meet us, so that added greatly to the significance of the event. We now understood why he referred to her as "doll face"; it was an apt description. As we got to know her better, it became increasingly apparent that her unique attractiveness included the reflection of a warm, sensitive and compassionate personality.

After meeting Helen, we no longer wondered why Pat wanted to come home every weekend, especially during the winter months. There was some risk, however, in making weekly trips and one Sunday evening on his return to Newton it came from an unexpected source. While passing through a desolate area of Pike County, a rear axle snapped in the Chevrolet, stranding him in the middle of that huge forest. Pat had become very proficient in replacing broken axles, but this time he had no spare axle in the trunk. Although the car would not move, he could start the engine from time to time to operate the heater and keep warm while he waited and hoped for assistance from a passing motorist. Not realizing that carbon monoxide was seeping into the car, he fell into a deep sleep, with the motor running. A state policeman on patrol noticed the idling car and Pat asleep in it. Immediately recognizing the dangerous situation that existed, he pulled Pat from the car and revived him in the cold air. The close brush with disaster did not change Pat's desire to return home each weekend to court Helen, but it did ensure repairs to the car's exhaust system and a steady supply of spare axles in the trunk.

With Pat working in Newton, I assumed much of the work at home that we had normally shared. Since I was now fourteen and getting bigger and stronger, the things I had to do were not overwhelming. There was, however, one task that was physically demanding and scary, one I never liked. It involved going into my grandfather's mine to replenish our home supply of coal. The opening of the mine was in a deep pit that existed since the time he tried to make coal mining on his land a commercial venture. The mine sloped down into the earth on a gentle grade and, for the first three hundred feet, was a classic mine. Carefully placed timbers supported the roof and sides. In the center of the floor, wide planks joined on the ends formed a runway for wheelbarrows, the vehicle for removing dirt and coal from the mine. Not finding a vein of coal after the first three hundred feet, my grandfather had dug an exploratory shaft to the left. It extended down for about six feet, with one shelf at the mid point. It was about four feet wide and, because of some solid rock support, lacked timbers or other bracing. Still not finding any coal, he decided to dig a small exploratory tunnel, which moved in the same direction as the main mine but six feet lower. The tunnel was about three feet wide and possibly forty inches high, big enough to get through on hands and knees and having enough clearance to keep from bumping a head on the roof. Like the shaft, the tunnel had no timbers or bracing. When the tunnel was about thirty feet long, he found a solid vein of coal, which turned out to be about five feet in height. Perhaps because the need for coal was immediate, he began removing it through the small tunnel and shaft and never extended the standard size main tunnel down to where the vein of coal began. I never knew why part of the mine remained undeveloped, but I suspect it had a lot to do with the extraordinary amount of physically demanding work it would take to properly complete it, and my grandfather was moving into his sixties when he began digging the mine.

By the time I became old enough, perhaps ten or eleven, to help Pat get coal from the mine, the removal of coal by various relatives had created a room in the mine that was twelve feet long, ten feet wide and five feet high. It had some supporting timbers, but not many. When I began entering the mine on my own, I always made certain the carbide lamp contained a full load of carbide and water, and I tested it to make sure it would easily light. I then placed the lighted lamp into the bracket on the front of a miner's cap I borrowed from my grandfather and started down the main tunnel. The really strong feelings of dread did not start until I reached the end of the main tunnel, made the long drop down the exploratory shaft, and began crawling on hands and knees toward the large room with the exposed face of solid coal. Inching down the cramped, damp tunnel we called the "rat hole" was the point at which I began my silent but serious praying. When I reached the room and coal vein, I would quickly begin digging chunks of coal from the vein with a pick or digging bar, tools that always remained in the mine. I worked at a furious pace, wanting to spend the least possible amount of time underground. When I dug the amount of coal I could handle for that day, I began tossing the chunks into that small tunnel, always acutely aware that I was blocking, at least partially, the only route of escape. I followed the coal into the tunnel and continued tossing it ahead of me until I reached the shaft and main tunnel. Though tired and wet from dripping mine water and sweat, I found it a great relief to be in the part of the mine that seemed reasonably safe.

Once the coal was outside the mine, it had to placed in large metal buckets, carried to the top of the pit, dumped into another wheelbarrow and wheeled home, a process that took at least six trips. At our home I accessed our coal bin by opening a basement window just below our kitchen and threw the chunks inside. The last remaining task in the process was to break the chunks into much smaller pieces before we used them. I always let that job wait for another day; it was time to get cleaned up and enjoy my survival.

While there were some areas of responsibilities that Ruth and I shared while my mother and Pat worked in Newton, she took care of Gene and the inside of the house and I did much of the outside work. This included cutting grass with our reel mower, a chore I enjoyed. I liked the soft, pleasant sound of the spinning reel, one that went as slow or as fast as I could move the mower. The smell of the freshly cut grass was one of the rewards for mowing. The same was true of the leaves we raked in the fall and hauled to a spot beyond our back yard and burned. For me, the aroma of burning leaves on an Indian summer day had a sense of nostalgia about it, a recognition that the beautiful, hazy days of fall would soon give way to the cold realities of winter. If I had not yet whitewashed the exposed outside basement walls, the harvest days reminded me that I should soon complete that job.

Frequently, Ruth would prepare a list of groceries we needed and I would walk to Whites Crossing, to Fedor's store, to get them. Since we always bought "on the book," I was sure to have that special book with me. It meant we were buying on credit. When Mr. Fedor, his wife or one of their children filled our grocery order, they wrote in our slender book the items that we bought, in what amount, at what price and the date we made the purchase. They recorded the same entry in a master book they kept. At least once a month my mother sent one of us to Fedor's store to pay what we owed. I was always quick to volunteer because, when I made a payment, they always filled a small brown bag with penny candy and gave it to me. Mr. Fedor was especially generous when he was available to take payments, and I always looked for him when I was there to pay our account.

Although it was his first formal job, Pat had much success in his work at Darlington Fabrics. He was a quick learner and, early in his employment, gave clear indications of a strong aptitude for mechanical and electrical work. He was progressing nicely at Darlington; his supervisors considered him an employee with significant promise, one the company wished to develop further. However, World War II was underway and, after working at Darlington just short of two years, Pat entered the United States Army on February 3, 1943. My mother would remain at her job in Newton until the fall of 1944, completing almost four years of weekend commuting while she worked at Darlington. Returning home permanently resulted from a job opportunity at a textile mill in Scranton, a job that was almost equal in pay to the one she had in New Jersey. Her homecoming was a joyful event for all of us because the weekend visits were much too brief, too filled with mundane necessities that she had to take care of before she left again. In going to Newton she had done what she had to do to support her family and retain her home, and her courageous and selfless sacrifice succeeded admirably.

In time I would come to understand how difficult it was for my mother to spend most of four years separated from her home and family. She missed many of the small things in family life that often become treasured memories, and she knew it. Her achievement takes on an even greater significance when one considers the price she paid in terms of personal happiness. The same is true of Ruth's exceptional performance in fulfilling a responsibility that infringed greatly on the days of her youth, but one she handled with a conscientiousness that never wavered. Life's heroes, it seems, frequently come forth from the most unlikely places, and most often they are not even aware of being in that role. And, while each of us in our own way paid our dues during those four long years, that's the way it had to be at that time and place.

CHAPTER **14**

Post Cards From the Past

❖◆❖

One of the special gifts that comes with youth is a natural resiliency, the ability to adapt to changing circumstances and to do things that are not the norm for young people. It appears nature intended a more gradual approach to the increasing challenges that come with young adulthood but, at the same time, provides the flexibility for children to deal with such challenges if and when necessary. The ability to assume certain activities normally reserved for adults does not, however, change the fact that children are still children. Though able to perform beyond their years when required to do so, they remain filled with a strong curiosity about their world and retain a desire to engage in games, have as much fun as possible, and occasionally find creative ways to get into mischief. So it was with us, and the area in and around Whites Crossing provided boundless opportunities to explore the good things in life and enjoy a multitude of activities, most of which we devised on our own.

―❖◆❖―

For about two years beginning in 1937, the Works Projects Administration worked on building a by-pass around Whites

Crossing. Known as the WPA, it was a federally funded program designed during the Depression years to employ those who could not find jobs. Prior to the by-pass construction, Route Six passed through Whites Crossing and continued up Number Four Road, past the school and the reservoir at the top of the mountain. The purpose of the by-pass was to avoid sending traffic through Whites Crossing and up that long, narrow and winding road. Construction of the by-pass started about three hundred feet from our home. Planned to sweep gradually over the Moosic Mountain range facing our home, the by-pass joined the older road close to Number Four Pond. In all, it was a two-mile by-pass, and we enjoyed watching from close range the construction of the new road.

When my father died, his old Model T Ford stood at the top of the hill behind our home, its restoration to running condition still far from completion. My mother began to give or sell parts of the Model T to those who needed them. By the middle of 1938, all that remained was the frame, four wheels with tires, the steering wheel, an empty gas tank, and the hand brake. It occurred to us that we happened to have the main parts of a car at a point where a newly paved road was not yet open to traffic. That seemed like a gift we simply had to use.

Pat and some of the older neighborhood boys moved the gas tank to a point near the steering wheel to serve as a seat, one close to the hand brake. When we were ready to take the Model T out for a ride, at least eight boys showed up to help push it uphill on the new concrete road. Without the motor and the body attached, it was surprisingly easy to move the chassis, especially with the number of boys eager to be passengers on the way down. Despite warnings from some grownups that we should not be taking the Model T out on the highway, it seemed like too good a thing to pass up. We pushed it uphill for more than a mile.

When we got to our starting point, we turned the car around

and Pat set the hand brake to hold the car in place while the gang found a spot on the frame to sit. Since we really wanted a fast ride, we designated a person to be a pusher once Pat released the brake. With encouragement from all of us, he ran down the road for about thirty feet pushing as hard as he could, then jumped aboard at the last possible moment. The remains of that old car moved at a brisk speed, helped, no doubt, by the combined weight of the delighted passengers. There was much yelling and shouting as we raced down the hill, and once we drifted to a stop near the Calafut house, we turned the car around and started back up the hill for another ride.

We enjoyed riding in that old car for about three weeks, until an event occurred that brought our fun to an abrupt end. Someone, with help from others, stole the remains of our old Model T. The parking spot at the top of the small hill behind our home, where the Model T stood for as long as I could remember, was empty. Seeing one morning that the car had disappeared was a depressing shock for all of us. Tire tracks through my grandparents' hay fields indicated that those who stole the chassis took it into Simpson. Though we never saw it again, we still treasure fond memories of that old Model T.

Over time the boys in most neighborhoods will select, almost unconsciously, a favorite home at which to gather. Most often, it is because they feel comfortable there; the location may be central to a lot of activity, and most important of all, the boys who live at that particular house are usually key members of the informal club. So it was in our neighborhood; the Calafut homestead was the unofficial headquarters for many of our gatherings, the planning and launching point for numerous adventures. Their home was across the street and to the left of ours, right on the edge of McDonald's hay field. It was a large, two-story home with a porch in front and another at the back. The grade of the land allowed for the basement door at the rear of the building to be at ground level. A few feet above the door was a rear porch, which provided a cover for the entrance to the basement. The entrance was also the access to their everyday kitchen, a place that served much like a clubhouse for all the boys who gathered there. The large lot extended from the edge of the road to a line of trees at the end of the property, a distance of approximately three hundred feet. Straight out from the basement door, most of the land on the right consisted of garden plots while a series of small sheds lined the left side. A well-worn path separated the sheds from the gardens and led into the woods behind the property.

The oldest of the three Calafut boys was Frankie, followed by Eddie and Johnny. All three had pleasant, easy going personalities, a trait that was also evident in their three older sisters, Sophie, Mary and Nellie. Their mother, a widow, must have passed on this special characteristic to her children because she had an exceptional tolerance for a group of boys constantly in her kitchen or just outside the door sitting on a bench and making a lot of noise. Occasionally, when things got out of hand, she would send us home, but that was rare. It did happen one evening when we decided to have a mini-war in their kitchen, with the lights out and using rubber bands and paper wads to shoot at each other. It was a large kitchen with many places to take shelter during the battle. We prepared well by cutting a piece of window screen to cover our faces, the screen held in place by cord. That was a good decision since some of the welts we received from wads fired at fairly close range were significant. The shouting, laughter, and cries of pain got louder as the war progressed.

When the invitation came from Mrs. Calafut to leave the kitchen, I was ready to go.

Early one summer, as we gathered at the Calafut homestead, we decided to build a pond, one we could use for many summers. We decided to build our pond by damming a stream that flowed from a reservoir called the New Dam, a reservoir hidden in the Moosic Mountains about three quarters of a mile from our homes. From the Calafut house we followed the path to the woods, turned right and continued on a path behind McDonald's hay field until we crossed over a stream that led to the one we planned to dam. The area was wide, open to the sun, and close to the abandoned railroad bed that stretched from Whites Crossing to Carbondale. We cleared rocks from the proposed swimming hole and, at the widest point, began to build a wall consisting of logs from fallen trees, stones, bags filled with a mixture of dirt and coal dust, and just about anything that would hold back enough water to make a swimming hole. It was hard work, a task that made me appreciate the physical strength of the older boys in our gang; they were always available to help when the smaller and younger members needed assistance in moving something heavy. In little more than a week, the swimming hole was holding water that was at least seven feet deep at the wall. It was about thirty feet across at its widest point and extended upstream for another forty feet. While the dam needed ongoing maintenance, it was one great swimming hole.

Eventually, we added a diving board to the wall where the water was deepest, although we used it more for jumping into the water than diving; there were still some rocks on the bottom. We also attached a rope to the limb of a large tree that extended to the center of the pond. There was usually a line of swimmers waiting for a turn to use the rope, for the riders swung high over the water and, dropping off, made a huge splash. The water was fairly cool since an artesian well was less than a hundred yards above the swimming hole and fed cold water into the stream at a constant rate. This gave us an excuse to frequently have a fire going when we were swimming. In addition, we were usually reluctant to walk back home to eat when we got hungry, so we would pick mushrooms that grew in the surrounding woods and roast them over the fire. The trick, of course, was to pick the right mushrooms. Folklore passed on by our elders told us what to look for, but I was never sure we knew what we were picking. We placed the plump mushrooms on sharpened sticks, held them over the hot coals until well done, and then ate them while they were still warm. It took a lot of mushrooms to satisfy a youthful hunger, and the fact that we all survived numerous feasts indicates we either got sound advice on what mushrooms to pick or we were very lucky. I still enjoy mushrooms to this day, but I don't recall ever eating any that tasted as good as those we picked in the nearby woods and carefully roasted over a camp fire beside that swimming hole.

The success we had in building that fine swimming hole started some discussion on the possibility of building a clubhouse, a place where we could meet, play games, tell stories, plan things to do, and even share some meals. Of course, it would be a private clubhouse, limited to members and, maybe, some special visitors. Allowing some visitors simply meant we wanted to be able to show it off, even though we had no idea how it would turn out. As our enthusiasm for the project increased, Eddie Calafut suggested we select a name for the club. Some members recommended some truly unusual names, and this led to many loud and lively exchanges. I don't recall how we reached a consensus, but everyone finally agreed the name would be "The Lucky Ten Boys Club." I am not at all certain, but I suspect the inclusion of the word "lucky" had something to do with our mushroom-picking skills.

The spot selected for the clubhouse was in a wooded area about fifty feet beyond the Calafut property line and close to a small stream. The location made sense: we were often in that area; and it was on the way to the swimming hole, the artesian well, and New Dam, a place where we liked to fish. We cleared out a large area, removing brush, small trees and stones, a job that did not go very fast since we could work at it only after we completed our responsibilities at home. Eventually, we cleared enough space to allow for a clubhouse that would be approximately ten feet long and eight feet wide. It looked much larger when we first marked it out on the ground, and the excitement began to mount as our project showed signs of becoming a reality.

We had no money to spend on the clubhouse, and that meant we would have to hunt for wood, nails, shingles, windows, a door, and anything else we might need. Much of the wood we used came from scraps found at the homes of club members. Other sources of wood included a community dumping area and donations from people who had old lumber on hand. I don't believe we used one new nail in the construction of that clubhouse. All were rusty nails pulled from old boards and straightened before being used again. Slowly, the clubhouse began to take shape. The studs were in place, the rafters added, and the side boards provided the strength to hold it together. We installed two small windows, one on each side of the building. After some trimming, we fit an old door into the doorway perfectly. On the outside, thin, narrow strips of wood nailed over the crevices between boards reduced the amount of cold air that might blow in. On the inside, clean cardboard nailed to the studs with roofing nails added some insulation and provided a neat, finished look.

As the clubhouse neared completion, we obtained an old table and an assortment of chairs for furnishings. We found a small potbellied stove to heat the clubhouse and persuaded some neighbors to part with some spare stove pipe to make a chimney. Finally, we added an old kerosene lamp for lighting and considered our clubhouse finished. It was very rustic looking, the old lumber adding a look of antiquity, but it was very solid and comfortable, as long as the winter weather was not bitterly cold. Being the youngest of the club members, I did not play a major part in the construction. My role was fetching, carrying, holding and, quite often, getting in the way. Whatever our contributions, we were all extremely pleased with the results.

Our parents were not entirely comfortable with our clubhouse; they worried that a group of boys gathering in a place such as that would surely get into trouble eventually. They had a point; we did get into mischief a few times. Perhaps it was more than a few times, but it only counted as mischief if we got caught. For the most part, it was a place to meet, talk, read comic books, play cards, argue and tell stories that had little basis in fact. The cabin could get much too hot at times, and if we used the kerosene lamp, the aroma that stayed on our clothing clearly announced to our parents where we had been. There was a very pleasant atmosphere about that cabin, resulting, I think, from the fact that it was something we planned and built together. It was ours, imperfect in some ways but a symbol of our camaraderie as boys and club members.

During one of our discussions at the clubhouse, someone suggested we could have some fun after dark by placing what appeared to be a new tire beside the road; specifically, the new by-pass taking traffic over the mountain. We reasoned it would be difficult for any motorists to resist picking up a new tire, even if it turned out to be one they could not personally use. The fun would begin when a motorist stopped, got out of the car or truck, and walked back to get the tire. The tire would disappear into the foliage alongside the road as soon as the vehicle began to stop, pulled there by tan baling cord attached to it.

At that time all new tires came tightly wrapped in brown paper; I don't know why, but that's the way auto stores sold them. Each tire resembled a large, brown donut. We found an old tire and, cutting brown paper bags into strips, we carefully wrapped the tire and glued the paper in place. It had the appearance of a brand new tire. We then tied a long piece of baling cord to the tire, trying to make it as inconspicuous as possible. When we were ready, we selected a spot along the road that was just above the abandoned railroad bed and less than two hundred yards from our clubhouse. The first night we tried our carefully planned deception, it worked exceptionally well. Drivers would quickly pull off the road as soon as they spotted the tire and hurry back to where they thought it should be, quite often accompanied by a passenger from the vehicle. Hidden in the trees and bushes, we enjoyed listening to their conversations as they tried to figure out what had become of the tire. We felt we had discovered the best source of entertainment since the invention of the radio.

Our prank began to attract the attention of some grownups in the area who would sit on a grassy hillside along the road to Whites Crossing and get a clear view of the action from a distance of about nine hundred feet. Having an audience spurred us on in the activity we enjoyed so much. Intent on putting on a good show, we never realized that after a few weeks we were beginning to fool some motorists for a second time. We recognized this when a driver, moving at a slow speed, suddenly veered his car toward our tire and stopped the vehicle with his right front wheel right on top of it. By the time he got out of the car, we were moving through the darkened forest at high speed, crossing the railroad bed and heading in the direction of the clubhouse. We got away, but he got our tire.

Since the new tire trick seemed to have run its course, we began to consider alternatives that would keep the fun going for us and amuse our audience on the grassy hillside. We settled on using a piece of iron from a broken car spring. Slightly curved, it was about three inches wide and fifteen inches long, and it made a loud, clanging noise when skipped across the road behind a moving car. With few exceptions, the cars would move to the side of the road upon hearing the noise, and driver and passengers would emerge to examine the car to find what had broken. Frequently, they would walk back toward our location looking for a part that they assumed had fallen from the car. They could not find the piece of iron we used since one of our club members on the opposite side of the road always picked it up. We were back in business.

One evening a state policeman stopped to talk to the grownups who were watching our little game. He strongly suggested they tell us to stop our activity since it posed some risk to travelers who stopped suddenly along a dark road to look for a problem that did not exist. We got the message, but we did not take the warning seriously. Traffic was usually very light, the shoulder along the new road was wide, and we saw no harm in continuing a fine prank.

About one week later, as we amused ourselves and our hillside fans, a fast-moving car suddenly swung toward our hiding place on the right side of the road; while the headlights shone on our startled faces, four state policemen leaped from the car and moved quickly toward us. We left the area in a big hurry, most of us running toward the railroad bed with the intent of crossing it, disappearing into the forest, and going to our cabin. Just as we reached the railroad bed, and before we could cross, a second police car pulled off the main road and started down the railroad right-of-way. It stopped as soon as we came in view, and more policemen joined the foot race. Not far away was a huge slag pile of waste from mining operations in the area. A loose mixture of slate, small stones and coal, it covered an area of about six acres and rose to a height of at least a hundred feet. Many of us instinctively started up the path toward the top since we played there frequently and knew that slag pile well. Running on that loose mixture was difficult because of the tendency to slip and slide as it gave way. The bouncing beams from flashlights held in the hands of pursuing policemen kept us strongly motivated to keep moving. The lights that played all around us as we ran gave the impression that they were a lot closer than they actually were. Reaching the top, we took different paths down the far side. By the time I reached the bottom, there was no longer a light on me and I was by myself.

One of the small talents I had then was the ability to run a long distance without stopping, but this was more use of that simple skill than I had ever wanted. I crossed the creek just below our swimming hole, angled toward the railroad bed, and headed in the direction of Carbondale. Eventually, I came to Brookside Street and followed that road until I crossed a pedestrian bridge at the foot of Canaan Street, just across the road from Russell's Ice Cream Parlor. I had run about two miles, and now I had to get back home. Thinking I would simply walk up Canaan Street, I suddenly realized that a sweaty, dirty, red-faced boy who was doing a lot of huffing and puffing would arouse the suspicion of policemen who might be patrolling the area looking for us. Crossing Canaan Street, I walked up a side street until it ended, then passed through back yards until I came to a wooded area that was parallel to the main road. Before too long I was in familiar territory, at the far edge of my grandparents' farm. I walked over the hay field we called the butley, passed by the rear of their garden, crossed behind Aunt Annie's home and entered our house through the back door. The lights were out and there was no one at home.

Undressing in the dark, I washed as best I could, drank at least a quart of water, and went to bed. I lay there straight and still, eyes wide open as I listened intently for a car that might stop at our house or the sound of footsteps coming up the front porch. There was little doubt in my mind that the policemen caught some of our club members and eventually we would all be rounded up. It was a long night, but nothing happened. It turned out that everyone got away. We realized how lucky we had been, and the incident reformed us to a great extent. Our attraction for occasional mischief did not diminish, but our days of agitating policemen were definitely over.

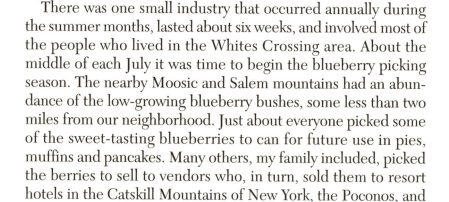

There was one small industry that occurred annually during the summer months, lasted about six weeks, and involved most of the people who lived in the Whites Crossing area. About the middle of each July it was time to begin the blueberry picking season. The nearby Moosic and Salem mountains had an abundance of the low-growing blueberry bushes, some less than two miles from our neighborhood. Just about everyone picked some of the sweet-tasting blueberries to can for future use in pies, muffins and pancakes. Many others, my family included, picked the berries to sell to vendors who, in turn, sold them to resort hotels in the Catskill Mountains of New York, the Poconos, and large hotels at other places. Although the berry picking season did not last long, it provided a source of income for the families who wanted to take advantage of the wild blueberry crop, and most families did.

Shortly before the picking season started, we made sure the two essential pieces of equipment were in order. One was a picking can, and everyone had a favorite. A wire handle attached to a coffee can to form a miniature pail was my preference. A belt around the waist held the can in place and allowed both hands to be free for picking berries. The second piece of equipment was one ten-quart bucket. As we filled each picking can, we carefully poured the berries into the larger container. The intent was to fill the ten-quart bucket, the picking cans and any secondary bucket we might bring along.

There were two reasons why we wanted to be on the mountain ready to pick berries as soon as darkness gave way to dawn. The main reason was that berry buyers would be at a designated spot near the mountain at eleven o'clock to buy berries, and they seldom stayed for more than a few hours. They wanted to get the berries to their customers as fast as possible, while the berries were still fresh. The second reason for an early start was to conclude the berry picking before the heat of the day reached its peak. As a result, we arose before daylight, ate a quick breakfast, took our utensils and headed to the mountains by way of Whites Crossing. As we walked through the dark up Number Four Road, the crowd would get larger. The grownups stayed together while the youngsters joined their friends in chattering, acting boisterously, or bragging about what a spectacular berry picking day was anticipated. Everyone, it seemed, had an idea where the largest crop of plump blueberries grew, a situation that made for easy, fast picking and top prices.

Being on the mountain near Number Four Pond as the sun came up and filtered through the mist rising from the water was reason enough to be there. As soon as it was light enough, groups of berry pickers scattered about the mountain, most staying close to a few friends as they moved about looking for berry bushes others had not yet found. Although people were frequently hidden from each other by mountain shrubs, their conversations were continual. Eventually, some would stray out of range and much calling back and forth took place, especially when a picking can overflowed with berries and someone else had the large bucket. A loud cry of anguish usually meant someone had the misfortune of spilling a can of newly picked berries, a small disaster since berry picking was not exactly easy. Because blueberry bushes tend to be quite low, we either picked from a stooped position or knelt on the ground to get the berries. I preferred the kneeling technique; it got me close to the work at hand and seemed a lot easier than bending over. It was also a way of getting the distinctive musty aroma of the mountain into my clothes, something that appealed to me. While the process had a somewhat serious purpose, the atmosphere was playful and good-humored.

There was always the risk of losing the good humor when it came time to sell the berries to the vendors. Blueberries have a soft blue patina that gives them a dry, powdery appearance. This is what the buyers wanted. Too much shaking of the freshly picked berries caused them to lose that ideal appearance; they took on a darker, almost wet look, which meant they were worth less. In addition, if we tended to get leaves and small twigs in with the berries, the buying price got lower still. If we got safely by those hurdles, the measuring process brought another challenge. The buyers would pour our berries into quart-size baskets, a means of determining the total purchase price since they paid by the quart. The quart baskets, rounded high with berries, seemed to be a standard form of measurement. This always led to complaints from pickers but rarely changed anything. The price paid for top quality berries was about nineteen cents a quart, while those on the lower end of the scale brought fifteen cents a quart. On a good day, Pat, Ruth and I would pick twelve quarts and take home two dollars and twenty-eight cents, a fairly decent amount then.

By one o'clock we were on our way home, usually satisfied with the berry picking results and already planning where we would go the next day to find an even better crop. There was a farm on the route to and from the Number Four Pond area that had a variety of blueberries called high huckles. This meant the berry bushes grew from four to six feet high and the fruit was often larger than that found on low bushes. Mrs. Bruning, owner of the farm, protected her fields by allowing a bull to roam free in a fenced-in area that contained the prized berry bushes. On our way home one day my group decided to visit Mrs. Bruning's high huckle patch. Approaching the field from nearby woods, we stood at the barbed wire fence for a long time, looking for any sign of the bull. Finally convinced he was in the barn, we crawled under the barbed wire and started to pick berries. The berries were large, the picking was easy, and we soon got more complacent than we should have been. When we first noticed the bull, he was about a hundred yards from us, looking surprised to see us in his field. He immediately broke into a trot, in our direction, while we all sounded the alarm and ran at full speed toward the fence, newly picked berries flying in all directions. Scrambling under the barbed wire, we headed into the woods and toward home, content to confine our berry picking to the relative safety of the mountains.

Just behind Costolnick's Tavern, on the right side of the road leading to Simpson, a swampy area called the Greenie Pond became one of our favorite places. The numerous small green frogs that lived in the pond inspired the name. During warm summer evenings they provided a continual chorus of unique sounds. However, it was a place we made use of only during the winter months when the pond froze. No part of the swamp was very deep, but a large section near the road was deep enough to cover rocks, swamp grass and other obstructions and make a clear area for ice skating. Much of the skating took place in the evening with a huge fire casting light across the frozen pond. Logs arranged around the fire served as a place for us to put on skates or take them off when it was time to go home. When it was bitter cold, getting a seat at the warm fire could be difficult. This was a popular place in the winter, and there was never a shortage of skaters for the games we played.

Hockey was a big favorite, and just about every boy had a carefully selected tree branch that matched a manufactured hockey stick in length and had a curve at the end that rested on the ice and controlled the puck. An empty condensed milk can crushed down to two inches in height served as a puck. The lack of fancy equipment did nothing to hamper the enthusiasm with which we played the game. At times I thought I would spend the rest of my life with bruised shins. Invariably, a game ended when someone had to go home to have some bleeding attended to.

Quite often the boys would join the girls in a skating exercise called Crack the Whip. The action required a lead skater who was skilled at skating backwards. The leader faced a line of eight to ten skaters, each holding on to the skater in front. He and the skater who faced him interlocked arms, and the line was ready to move. As the lead skater moved backward, the entire line skated as hard as possible to build up speed. Nearing the end of the pond, the leader, moving swiftly backward, would suddenly turn sharply and stop, causing the whole line to swing in a great arc. Those at the end of the line picked up even more speed and few remained standing when the whip cracked. Often, one or more from the end of the line would slide across the ice in a sitting position and stop only when they hit something. Of course, everyone wanted a turn at the end of the line, and that kept the game going until we grew too tired to make another run.

On one side of the pond, where the swamp extended back into some woods, the frozen water created icy pathways through swamp grass and around rocks and logs protruding above the surface. It was always nice to take a break from more vigorous skating and just glide along the frozen trails, which wandered through the swamp and eventually led me back to where I had started. The winter gave the swamp in this particular area a unique landscape, a kind of quiet charm. None of the frozen waterways were straight; they meandered, twisted, turned and interconnected, forming an icy maze. Many of the trees that once grew there were now dead and, shorn of any limbs, stood like sentinels keeping watch over this little patch of wilderness. Snow covered the rocks and logs that rose above the ice and clung to dry swamp grass that swayed in the cold wind. This was a place best enjoyed alone, with just the whispery sound of my skates cutting into the ice as I glided slowly through the moonlit swamp. Long after I no longer skated at the Greenie Pond, I would mentally visit that place and smile at the pleasant memories.

Sledding was also a big part of our winter recreation, and Number Four Road provided the best possible hill for that sport. When the road remained covered with a blanket of packed snow, just about every boy and girl old enough to be outdoors without parents would be sledding down that hill, usually in the evening. In groups we walked uphill to a point close to Robert Morris School, the starting point for going down the steepest part of the hill. It was a long, fast ride with a few curves along the way to make it really interesting. We would fly by Rushen's store, pass Louie Novobilski's tavern, speed over the old railroad bed, begin to slow down near Kresock's Tavern and come to a stop at Fedor's store. It was a great ride, long and fast, the kind that made my eyes water from the wind in my face as I raced downhill.

Basically, children had two kinds of sleds, Flexible Flyers and Lightning Guiders, and there were always debates over which was the faster. Since ours was a Lightning Guider, there was no doubt in my mind about who had the fastest sled. In addition, I would argue, we always sanded our runners to make them as smooth as possible and then applied a coat of wax to the metal. It remained a never-ending point of contention, however, since all sledders felt they had the ideal way to make their sled the fastest. On one point we all agreed: the fastest thing to come down that huge hill was a homemade sled called the Bull Giant.

There is reason to believe that Joseph Zukowski, our next door neighbor and oldest son in that family, built the Bull Giant. He made a fearsome machine. The sitting area, a large plank two inches thick, twelve inches wide and eight feet long, connected to front and rear runners. The runners, shaped from wood to resemble the front end of a sled, had metal attached to the bottom edges to produce speed. The rear runner remained fixed in place while the front runner moved, allowing the Bull Giant be turned and steered by pulling on ropes fastened to the left and right sides. Attached to the bottom of the plank were pieces of metal on which riders could place their feet when they sat on the Bull Giant and held on for a downhill ride. When tightly packed with riders, it held at least six people, including the driver. It was the weight of the Bull Giant and its riders that made it so fast. It was not only fast, it made a loud, distinctive sound as it sped downhill, a sound that caused every youngster on the hill to shout the alarm that the Bull Giant was coming. Not easily steered, the large, heavy sled needed a lot of space and justified the loud warnings that it was coming downhill.

I had my share of rides on the Bull Giant, and each was comparable to a ride on a rocket that was not entirely under control, at least not from my perspective. While the ride was always a wild, exhilarating experience, getting off at the bottom of the hill without crashing was also a joyful happening. The crashes that occurred with the Bull Giant included running off the road or turning over, most often because the driver was trying to avoid hitting something. Concerned with the potential for injury, the parents in the village frequently voiced their lack of appreciation for our magnificent machine. The end for the Bull Giant came in the third year of its use. Loaded with boys, the Bull Giant was approaching the bottom of the hill when disaster struck. The driver attempted to turn up the old railroad bed while still traveling at great speed. The Bull Giant began to skid sideways and slammed into a pole, breaking the leg of a rider. Within days it disappeared and we were back to normal sledding, which seemed sedate and tame when compared to the wild rides on the Bull Giant.

The two reservoirs in the mountains close to our home, New Dam and Number Four Pond, were owned by a major water company. Large and well maintained, both had areas of grass near the retaining walls that had the appearance of well-kept lawns. Clean and free of debris, both were inviting mountain lakes. In all respects they were model reservoirs, and that, most likely, was one reason why posted signs around the reservoirs discouraged fishing. Security personnel from the water company routinely toured both dams to inspect the property and apprehend trespassers. While that did a lot to discourage fishing, many still felt tempted to try their luck discreetly since the fishing was usually very good at both places. I was among those who could not resist the attraction.

The first bamboo fishing pole I could call my very own came from Fedor's store. They had at least two dozen stacked in a little offset at the left front of the building, behind a wrought iron fence. This was an important purchase for me, so I took a long time searching for just the right pole. I must have examined each one at least three times before selecting one that was long, slender and straight. I also bought a spool of standard green fishing line and a few fishhooks. All I needed was a bobber to let me know when a fish was nibbling at the bait, and a large cork I had at home would serve that purpose. I was ready to go fishing.

On a warm Sunday afternoon, armed with our fishing gear and a small can of bait, five of us headed toward New Dam. We followed the path that went by our clubhouse, the swimming hole, and the artesian well beyond the railroad bed. From there we walked up the steep left rim of the huge ravine leading to the dam. When we emerged from the woods, we were at the foot of the stone and cement retaining wall, a wall that rose for eighty-five feet and was at least two hundred feet long at the top. Blocking that deep, narrow ravine created a large, beautiful mountain lake.

Since it was Sunday and we did not expect to see any security guards at the dam, we casually walked up the grassy slope near the stone wall. At the top of the wall we looked in all directions for any sign that a guard patrolled the dam. Seeing no evidence that a security guard was in the area, we elected to walk across the crest of the broad stone wall and fish on the right side of the dam, about a hundred yards from the wall. This gave us a clear view across the dam, especially the large, open area from which a guard was most likely to approach. In a short time bobbers were floating above baited hooks in the sunlit water while our fishing poles rested in small, V-shaped branches we cut from trees and stuck in the ground. The supports kept the long bamboo poles about three feet above the water to avoid having the bobbers pulled under the surface by the weight of the poles.

The perch were biting that particular day, and in about two hours we had about ten or twelve fish. We placed them on stringers, tied the stringers to some driftwood and placed the fish in the water. As often happens when a group is fishing, two in our party felt they could be more successful if they moved to a better spot along the shoreline. Taking their poles and a supply of bait, they began to follow a narrow path that led toward the rear of the dam. Barely five minutes after leaving, they came rushing back to tell us they had spotted a security guard headed our way. Instead of coming in to the dam area from the main entrance near the wall, this security guard had driven past the dam, parked near the inlet, and begun patrolling from the far end of the reservoir. The obvious intent was to surprise any fishermen who might be trespassing. Except for our two friends looking for a more productive fishing area, the surprise maneuver would have worked to perfection.

Yanking our bamboo poles from the water and leaving the bait and stringers of fish behind, we hurried into the woods and moved away from the shoreline. Shouts from the security guard let us know he saw us and increased our desire to get away. Unfortunately, this was our first experience with rushing through woods and shrubs with ten-foot fishing poles. Worst yet, we did not have time to wind the fishing line around the poles and anchor the hooks into the base. I covered less than fifty feet before my line and hook snagged on a bush. With one mighty tug I succeeded in breaking the line; I did not want to lose my new fishing pole. Eventually, we all found our way back to the swimming hole where we discussed our bad luck and lost fish. My biggest regret was that I would not be eating perch coated in eggs and flour and fried until crispy brown by my mother.

I continued to use my bamboo fishing pole when my Uncle Joseph took neighborhood children to places like Lake Ladore and Keen's Pond. It was always fun and the fishing was usually good. It did lack, however, the challenge of fishing at the restricted reservoirs. As a result, our gang continued to fish at New Dam and Number Four Pond, especially when we found we could catch fish by using a line, hook, and the right bait. Anchoring one end of the line to a stone near the shore, we would carefully coil the rest of the line on a flat rock. Then, loosely wrapping the line near the hook around a small stone, we would toss the stone as far out into the water as we could. It would carry the line with it and fall away as the line sank into the water with the bait. We caught some fine-looking fish using this method. If we saw a security guard approaching, we simply faded into the woods after pushing the anchor rock into the water and out of sight. When the guard left, we would retrieve the line, often with a fish attached. We had a lot of fun at the two reservoirs, and it was years later that I realized I never knew of anyone caught by a security guard at either location. It dawned on me that perhaps it was never their intent to catch us; just getting us to leave may have been their goal. Fishing there would have been a lot less fun if we had known that at the time.

After the smaller of the two elementary schools burned to the ground in 1937, the larger and newer building continued to serve the community for another twenty-two years. Robert Morris School was a one-story, flat roof building with a basement that housed the heating plant, coal and some supplies. It had a long, wide hallway that separated the classrooms, three on the left and one on the right. Oil applied to the wooden floors each summer helped to preserve the wood and keep dust to a minimum during the school year. The desks, made of wood mounted on black metal frames, stood anchored to the floor in neat rows. Each desk came equipped with a shelf below the writing surface for the storage of books and tablets. One wall in each classroom had large windows that let in generous amounts of light and provided a good view of rain and snow storms. Lining two of the walls, one to the front of the room and one to the right, were blackboards. A novel convenience for just about every student were the inside rest rooms, something that was not standard at most homes. A single pencil sharpener mounted in the hallway completed the basic school necessities.

Surrounding the building was a lot of open space for playing during recess, including a baseball field at the rear of the building. To the left of the building, beyond the open play area, was a patch of hilly woods containing a web of well-used paths, evidence that scores of students over the years found this a favorite place to run and play. For most students the two recess periods were the highlights of the day, a time to be noisy, tease the girls, talk, run and always complain about how quickly recess ended. At lunch time and at the end of the school day I usually left for home on the run. Crossing the ball field near home plate, I'd run down a short hill, skip across a small stream by landing on three stones just right and continue through a stand of white birch trees until I reached Route Six, just above the old railroad bed. From that point the distance to our home was not too great, but I rarely slowed the pace. I always enjoyed that run, even after I missed one of the rocks while crossing the stream one day and fell into the water. While I liked running that short cut on the way home, I usually walked to the school through Whites Crossing and up Number Four Road, accompanied by an ever-growing group as we neared that old gray building.

Although all the basics of education filled our days during the first few years, it seemed that learning the multiplication tables received particular attention. We played games using flash cards, teams competed against each other, and daily drills tested our skills. Above the top edge of the blackboards in classrooms for the first four grades the "times tables" remained on continual display. By the time students moved to the fifth grade, just about everyone could instantly give the answer to any multiplication problem beginning with two times one and ending with twelve times twelve. The rote memory of the tables established a high level of confidence with arithmetic, the common name for mathematics at the time, and provided a sound basis for solving problems at a more complex level. It was a segment of education that became indelibly imprinted on the brain and provided a lifetime of service.

One of the challenges we faced in our school life at Robert Morris occurred when a teacher requested that we go to a blackboard to demonstrate our understanding of arithmetic, spelling, English, geography and other subjects. The teacher would start by asking for volunteers, and there were always a few who would raise an arm and vigorously wave for the right to show their skills, whether or not they had any. The rest of us would suddenly be very busy looking intently, with heads down, at some paper on our desks while we fervently wished for a few seconds of invisibility. In going to the blackboard, we had an even chance of looking like either a scholastic hero or the class idiot before our peers; those odds did not inspire the more rational students to volunteer. Eventually, of course, our turn came to go to a blackboard and confirm, orally and in writing, our knowledge about a particular subject. Sometimes it went very well while at other times it was ten minutes of slow death, especially when we had to diagram a sentence and describe the function of each word. Being ready for class was always the best defense since the teachers had an uncanny instinct for knowing when we failed to do our homework.

There was at Robert Morris a remarkable continuity in the teaching staff, which for some families meant three generations could discuss having been taught by the same teacher. The teachers with the greatest number of years at Robert Morris also lived in the Whites Crossing community. They shopped at the local stores, attended the same churches and knew most families on a personal basis. As neighbors and active members of the community, they were there to rejoice at christenings, mourn at wakes, and take part in all the special celebrations that fall between the coming and going of life. This long, close involvement with the families of Whites Crossing gave them a unique perspective on each child who came into their classrooms.

Among the teachers who served at Robert Morris, three had long, distinguished careers at that location. Their combined years of teaching in that elementary school most likely exceeded by far the total of all others who may have taught there. Mary McDonald, her sister, Ruth, and Mary Fox Telep became so closely identified with the school it almost seemed they came with the building. It was not unusual for former students of all ages to share recollections of days spent in the classrooms with those three outstanding individuals. Often, it was a comparison of stories regarding teaching techniques, habits and personalities. Many would also recount being compelled to stay after classes because of some misbehavior during the day. Without exception, there was strong agreement among former students that the three were fair, firm, dedicated and rarely fooled by student ploys, most likely because they had seen them all numerous times.

Mary McDonald had the added responsibility of being the school principal and the distinction of having taught at Robert Morris for forty years. During this time, I suspect her approach to her job remained unchanged. Serious and concerned, she used her total knowledge of each student's background to shape her approach to each pupil's particular needs. More than anything

Mary McDonald
Robert Morris School Principal

else, she was a very caring and compassionate lady. One of her special talents was the ability to see each of her pupils as a unique individual and, even though she was conducting two classes within the same room, she never seemed to lose track of anyone. She, more than other teachers, had the opportunity to teach parents, their children, and their grandchildren. The number of young lives she influenced during their formative years is extraordinary, and many went on to realize the promise she saw and carefully nurtured in them. While she never married or had children of her own, it seems she had a full, satisfying life helping to raise the children of Whites Crossing. In all, her career spanned forty-seven years, all but seven at Robert Morris School. As the school population declined in the area and the building of larger and more modern schools took place at other locations within the school district, Robert Morris School closed. At closure, Miss McDonald was the only remaining teacher in the building. Somehow, it seemed appropriate that she was the last to leave; after all those years, it really was her school to close.

Once every summer an event took place that was the highlight of the year for many children in the Whites Crossing, Simpson and Carbondale areas. Known as Kiddies' Day at Newton Lake, the site for the grand affair was an amusement park located about four miles north of Carbondale. Newton Lake was also a resort locality for the few who could afford to build cottages along the shoreline. The swimming area had an extensive sandy beach and that added to the popularity of the lake. Built along the eastern shore of the lake, the amusement park was a major attraction but one we rarely got to visit. Going to an amusement park for a day of fun was not high on the family list of priorities when it came to spending money. The same was true for most families at that time. As a result, when the merchants of Carbondale and Simpson sponsored the annual visit to Newton Lake, it was a significant happening for hundreds of children from the area. For many it compared favorably to having a day like Christmas during the warmth of summer.

Besides providing tickets for a variety of rides at Newton Lake, the merchants made certain each child also had tickets for soda, hot dogs and ice cream. My mother, realizing we were prone to be hungry about every half hour, would also pack a lunch for each of us to take along. The aroma of bologna sandwiches in each bag, mingled with that of a banana and orange, added a lot to the adventure of the day. Somehow, she always managed to find a few coins to give us, enough for each of us to buy an extra ice cream cone or soda. Her enthusiasm for the event was as great as ours. We did not realize at the time how much pleasure it gave her to see us go on a one-day vacation to Newton Lake, a vacation she could not have afforded on her own.

The fun of the day started with the trip to Newton Lake. Stake-bodied trucks, provided by the sponsors of Kiddies' Day, transported the children and their chaperons to the lake. Hanging on while the truck bounced along the road, the wind blew apart our carefully combed hair as everyone laughed and talked at the same time. That trip to the park set the tone for the day and raised our anticipation to an even higher level. It was in every sense the first great ride of that special day, and we could look forward to it being the last ride of the day when we returned home at dusk.

Once the truck parked, we wasted no time jumping to the ground, lunch bags clutched in one hand while the other checked to make certain our allotment of tickets were still safe in a pocket. As we hurried toward the amusement area, the sounds and the activities taking place created a sense of excitement that would last all day. The noise from the rides, colored lights, music from the carousel, and the smell of cooking food provided a wondrous atmosphere for the annual visit to Newton Lake. Wanting to enjoy everything, we often found it difficult to pick a starting point. Some liked the Whip, others the Caterpillar or Roller Coaster. Pat favored the Dodge-Em cars and Ruth enjoyed everything except the Roller Coaster. Having youthful visions of being a cowboy someday, I really liked the Carousel. Selecting my favorite horse, always on the outside edge, I rode far beyond the circle made by the Carousel.

Since we wanted to space our rides to avoid being out of tickets before the end of the day, we took time to watch people try to win prizes by knocking things down, enjoyed a hot dog or soda, watched the swimmers at the beach, and terrified people going down the steepest drop on the Roller Coaster. The sponsors of Kiddies' Day also organized a series of games for the children and awarded prizes to the winners. Even when we did not take part, it was great fun to watch games like a sack race, wheelbarrow race and pie-eating contests. When it came to pie-eating, it was always hard to tell the winners from the losers. At some point we would find a picnic table under a shade tree and begin eating the lunch our mother had packed for us. By the end of the day no tickets remained for rides or food. The last ride taken, our coins spent and the lunches eaten, it was time to go home. We felt pleasantly tired, looked a bit dusty, and the front of my shirt made it evident that I had eaten well and often. The slow pace of our walk back to the trucks that would take us home showed our reluctance to see the day end; the next Kiddies' Day was a long way off. On the ride home the children seemed subdued and pensive as each privately relived the joys of the day and stored memories that would last a lifetime, a generous gift from good people we did not really know.

CHAPTER **15**

While Waiting For a War

◆◆◆

When I was about eleven, I happened to be visiting the Calafut homestead when one of the boys invited me to go up to the attic to look for something, an item I no longer recall. A finished staircase led from the second story of the house to a fully floored attic. It was a very charming attic, one that received a lot of light from a dormer at the front of the house. While there, I discovered some fine-looking books in a box against the wall. The hard blue covers with titles imprinted in gold gave the books an elegant appearance. It was obvious they were a set of classic books. From that brief visit to the Calafut attic, I became seriously addicted to reading. Many times I would place four or five green apples in a brown bag, along with a salt shaker, walk to the Calafut home and ask for permission to go to the attic to read books. Eating salted apples as I read, I spent hours being entranced by *Robinson Crusoe, Huckleberry Finn, Treasure Island, Tom Sawyer, Kidnapped, Ivanhoe* and other great stories. The reading habit that blossomed in an attic soon spread to anything printed. It was not possible to be near newspapers or magazines such as *Collier's* without picking them up to read. My world became a lot bigger.

The growing war in Europe began to capture everyone's attention and I soon became caught up in what was taking place. I followed the headlines, read the stories, listened to radio reports, and looked forward to going to the movies because, besides the feature film and a cartoon, there was usually a filmed report on world news. The pictures of the war were fascinating, even while they created a sense of uneasiness. Once again the German military machine was on the move, Europe was in turmoil and the wrong side was winning. Technically, our country was neutral, but certainly not in thought or sympathy. Many of our elders had come from the lands now being conquered by Hitler's armies and almost all still had relatives in the affected countries. Their concerns grew as country after country fell under the domination of Germany. Being young and idealistic, I could not understand why we as a nation were not helping our friends as we had in the previous European war.

While the war in Europe continued to spread, life at home seemed to continue at a normal pace. It appeared we really were going to remain neutral. Between news reports on the war, we continued to listen to our favorite stories on the radio, stories made exceptionally real because our imaginations supplemented the words of the actors and created spectacular images of the action taking place. We rode throughout the West with the Lone Ranger and Tonto, traveled with Jack Armstrong on weekly adventures, and marveled at the ability of the Shadow to remain unseen as he solved mysteries and captured the bad guys. Comedy shows were also popular and we rarely missed listening to Jack Benny, Amos 'n' Andy or George Burns and Gracie Allen. The best shows came on in the evening, and the soft yellow glow from the dial added a distinctive charm to the entertainment, especially when we sat in a dimly lit room with family and friends and enjoyed a night of great radio programs.

The Irving Theater in Carbondale showed the finest filmed news reports. Produced by Pathe News or Paramount Studios, the reports' vivid scenes showed the horror of the war in Europe, revealing the might of the German Army and the suffering of the conquered people. Newsreels on the Japanese invasion of China were similar in many respects to those on Germany's invasion of neighboring countries. The scenes and the rapid-fire speaking style of the news commentator seemed to suggest an urgent need to take some action. As we watched the reports in glum silence, there was a growing conviction that, despite our official neutrality, it was unlikely we could remain out of the conflict. There were many times when I left the theater thinking more about the newsreels than the movie.

The Irving Theater was a truly elegant movie house that showed first run movies featuring the finest actors in Hollywood. It was a broad theater with curving rows of seats on the first floor and red velvet drapes framing the screen. On the second floor, a large balcony provided clear viewing. To the rear of the balcony, a luxurious sitting area accommodated those who wished to sit and visit while waiting for the featured film to start. At the very front of the balcony, a special section of deluxe seating called loges attracted young couples. The seats were large and plush, the view was unobstructed, and the carpeting was soft and deep. Of course, it cost a bit extra to sit in the loge area, but for those who wanted to make a serious impression on a young lady, it was the only way to go. As a rule, the boys went to the Majestic Theater with their buddies to see cowboy movies, talk loudly and act a bit rowdy. The atmosphere at the Irving inspired better behavior, as did the scope and quality of the movies shown there, such as *Gone With the Wind*, *Grapes of Wrath*, *Robin Hood* and *Boys' Town*. Each theater had its place in the community, but going to the Irving was more than a movie experience; it was a brief contact with a touch of class.

On September 1, 1939, Germany used its superior air power and ground forces to begin the invasion of Poland. Despite serious protests from France and Great Britain, the invasion continued at a swift pace and the entire country was soon under German control. For the many Polish families in our area, including my grandparents, their worst fears had become a reality. On September 3, 1939, France and Great Britain declared war on Germany and the war moved to a new level. Our hopes for an end to Hitler's conquests faded quickly as German troops began the invasion of France and the bombing of Great Britain. In May 1940, Winston Churchill became Prime Minister of Great Britain and made a sobering assessment of the situation when he declared in his first speech as Prime Minister, "I have nothing to offer but blood, toil, tears and sweat." In June 1940, hundreds of British civilians with boats crossed the English Channel to help the British Navy rescue 340,000 British troops trapped at Dunkirk, France. In my young mind it was the greatest rescue that had ever taken place, and there was some cause for optimism. However, when Paris fell to the Germans in the same month and the German influence continued spreading all over mainland Europe, the situation became increasingly grim. As a country we were still not a part of the conflict, despite our strong sympathies for the countries falling under the domination of Germany. However, as conditions in Europe continued to worsen, there was a very real sense that we were edging closer to war.

During the Great Depression, before activities relating to war caused a significant improvement in the economy, large numbers of men roamed the country seeking a few days of employment wherever they could find it. Sleeping along the roadways, under bridges, or in abandoned shacks, they seemed to belong to no one and had no permanent home. Their tattered, patched and soiled clothing reflected the rough conditions under which they existed. Their unshaven faces had a dark bronze color, caused by a combination of sun, wind, and a lack of frequent washing. Many had a look of sad hopelessness, a condition that likely came from long months of searching, without success, for a better life. We called them "bums" or "hoboes," but not in a derogatory sense; the names were more a description of what they did to survive. Living along a main road, we saw them on a fairly regular basis during the summer and fall of the year. When they stopped at our home, or at other places along the road, it was to ask for something to eat.

Usually traveling alone, a hobo would walk up our driveway to the porch at the rear of the house and knock on the screen door. If any of the children answered the knock, we quickly summoned our mother, who took the simple request for food and water. Without fail, she fed every bum or hobo who came to our door and asked for food. While a hungry man sat on the top step of the porch eating a sandwich, soup or a bowl of stew, we children stood in the background and watched, filled with curiosity about this scruffy-looking stranger. There was seldom much conversation; most seemed too weary to talk. Before our visitors left, my mother often gave them a bag containing food. Upon leaving, their expressions of gratitude were brief but sincere.

Not everyone agreed with what my mother was doing. Some suggested some kind of marking or code known only to a bum or hobo was guiding them to our door because of her generosity. It didn't matter; it simply was not in her character to turn away a person in need. She never attempted to make her actions a kind of lesson in life for us or consciously use them to set an example. The fact is she did it because caring was a deeply ingrained part of her character and personality. For her, sharing with someone in need, even when we had little to share, was the right thing to do.

While we watched and waited, the war in Europe began to get more desperate for the side we favored. President Roosevelt began formulating plans to assist Great Britain, at least with war equipment, but the country was generally unaware of that. The person who continually raised the hopes of his country, and ours as well, was Winston Churchill. Rotund, almost bald, short in stature, his face an expression of pugnacious determination, in appearance he was a most unlikely hero. His eloquence, however, supported by the strength of his will, gave hope when none seemed possible and repeatedly he rallied his people to fight on. National radio broadcasts of his recorded speeches never failed to inspire, to instill hope that Great Britain would hang on and eventually triumph. Following the evacuation of British troops from Dunkirk, Churchill's remarks inspired freedom-loving people everywhere when he said, "Wars are not won by evacuations…we shall fight on the seas and oceans…in the air,…on the beaches,…in the streets,…in the hills,…we shall never surrender." Delivering his speech in a voice that was part-growl, but also defiant and confident, he was extremely persuasive, a leader who made the British and many others believe in his message. The Royal Air Force, gallantly defending their island nation and continually frustrating German plans to invade Great Britain, symbolized the many in that nation who heard Churchill's words and translated them into action. At the time we also needed a hero directly involved in the war and Churchill fitted the role to perfection. It was becoming increasingly obvious, however, that he was going to need some help.

The children in our family had limited sources for obtaining spending money since most earnings went into a common family fund. However, we usually received a share of the berry picking money and a bit from the paper route income. Occasionally, relatives would pay a small amount for specific work they needed done, and we frequently collected scrap iron and sold it to junk dealers who came by on a regular basis and paid a few cents for each pound of iron. It was possible to accumulate a small amount of coins and spend them on things we really wanted. Since my mother usually supplied movie money, I spent my small cache of coins on good things to eat. I had a particular fondness for chili hamburgs or hot dogs with "everything on"; onions, mustard and chili. The hot chili, always liberally applied, slid down the sides of the bun and covered a large portion of the plate. That tasty meal, accompanied by steaming hot coffee, fortified me many times for the walk up Canaan Street after I'd seen a movie in a Carbondale theater.

There was some debate about which restaurant served the best chili hamburgs and hot dogs, and the three contenders for that honor were the Carawanna, Elite and the Crystal. For a long time I favored the Carawanna, a long narrow restaurant on Salem Avenue. I may have been partial to it because the opening date above the door, chiseled in stone, matched my birth year. It was by far the smallest of the three restaurants, and as customers entered, they brushed by those seated at the counter just inside the door. A collection of booths at the end of this oversized hallway provided some cramped seating. Despite its small size, business was always brisk. Across the street and up near the end of the block was the Crystal, the place I came to prefer. It was larger, open, bright, more comfortable and a seat was usually available. All three restaurants had a similar aroma, which caused instant hunger as I entered. The smell of chili, onions, garlic and hot coffee was like a friendly welcome, an assurance that I'd come to the right place. When I lacked the funds for a hamburg, I'd stop at Russell's Ice Cream Parlor at the foot of Canaan Street to spend five cents on a huge double dip cone and eat it slowly as I walked uphill.

By the fall of 1940 Congress enacted legislation designed to prepare the country for the potential of war by drafting men into the armed services. Near the end of October a lottery took place to initiate the draft by drawing the numbers of those destined to be the first draftees. A one year training period was the standard. Many, choosing not to wait for the call to arms, elected instead to volunteer for a year of service and put that obligation behind them. The entire process, reported extensively in the news, focused attention on the war and emphasized the likelihood that we could become involved in the conflict. One of the first to be called was Johnny Klickus, the oldest son of our Aunt Annie. Since he lived next door, the reality of the draft took on greater significance. Many continued to believe that the draft was simply a precaution, that being prepared to fight meant we could avoid doing so. One of the more popular songs at that time was "Good-by, Dear, I'll Be Back In a Year (for I'm In the Army Now)." Draftees and volunteers left for training camps by the thousands while we cheered them on, pleased that we were finally doing something.

WHILE WAITING FOR A WAR ◆ 155

The newspapers, magazines and newsreels began to cover extensively the preparations our country was taking for possible involvement in the war. Many events appeared to come rapidly. The Willys Overland Corporation, under contract with the government, produced the first Jeep in December 1940, a vehicle that every boy dreamed of owning someday. In February 1941, President Roosevelt requested that Congress pass a Lend Lease program to assist nations fighting the Germans. The law would permit the United States to lend all kinds of war equipment to our friends, with a special emphasis on warships, fifty of which went to Great Britain. As it turned out, he was requesting a law for something he had secretly authorized on his own about six months before, an event that pleased most who learned of it. It was comparable, he suggested, to "lending a hose to your neighbor when his house is on fire." In addition, British warships needing fuel or repairs had permission to use United States ports. In return for the fifty destroyers lent to Great Britain, the United States leased six naval bases in the British West Indies. In an agreement with the Dutch, our country accepted Greenland to protect it from the Nazis. A short time later, similar arrangements with Iceland made it appear that all these measures helped to establish defensive positions outside the continental United States. Meanwhile, promotion of the first Savings Bonds began in April, 1941 and sales were brisk. Seeing investments in Savings Bonds as a patriotic way of the getting the country ready for possible conflict, the public response exceeded all expectations. The materials needed to train armed forces personnel and arm them adequately spurred the economy and the demand for workers increased. We were not sure where all this was taking us, but it was clear that, for good or bad, times were changing.

When Germany attacked Russia in July 1941, and became engaged on two war fronts, we took that as a positive sign for our friends in Europe. It did not seem possible for a country with its resources spread to such an extent to succeed in a war. However, initial German successes suggested that yet another country would soon fall under its domination. The grim outlook began to change when an early Russian winter set in and the Russians remained undefeated. In a costly and bitter struggle, the Russians slowly brought the German invasion to a stop. Ill-prepared to fight in the hostile winter environment, the Germans were receiving strong indications of possible defeat on the eastern front. The intense war activities taking place all over Europe dominated the headlines and gripped our attention. There was an awareness of problems in the Pacific and Japan's aggressive moves to expand its influence and territory, but the issues did not seem to be that critical, especially when compared to the war being waged by Germany on so many of its neighbors. In addition, there seemed to be a belief that diplomats would resolve the problems existing between our country and Japan. As a result, our attention focused more intently on the war in Europe. Distracted by what we perceived to be a greater danger, most of us were looking in the wrong direction when disaster struck at Pearl Harbor.

December 7, 1941, came on a Sunday. Immediately after lunch I walked to the Calafut house to visit with the boys and look over the books in their attic that I had not yet read. It was probably close to three o'clock in the afternoon when one of the Calafut girls turned on the radio and heard the news of the attack on Pearl Harbor. As we huddled around the radio listening in silence to the description of the air attack on our ships and airfields, there was a sense of unreality about it. The impact of the news was so intense it created a tendency to disbelieve what we were hearing. I quickly left to spread the news, thinking those at home may not be aware of what had taken place. As I hurried along the roadway, I tried to make some sense out of what had happened, but nothing eased the overwhelming feeling of loss and confusion. We were the good guys, and things such as this were not supposed to happen to us. I had not felt this bad since my father died, so it was good to be heading home.

Our radio was on when I got home and my family, like most other Americans, appeared stunned. Within days we would see pictures of the burning ships, airplanes destroyed while still on the ground, wounded servicemen, and devastation all around the base at Pearl Harbor. These scenes became a backdrop against which our losses forever became etched: five battleships, fourteen smaller ships, two hundred aircraft, two thousand four hundred killed, and thirteen hundred wounded. The surprise attack numbed the entire country, especially when it became known that the enormous losses were caused by only three hundred and sixty Japanese planes flying from aircraft carriers. Shaken by both the attack and the fact we had been badly weakened, people gathered in groups to discuss the events and wonder if additional attacks might take place. It took a little longer for most people to understand that the intent of the attack was to neutralize United States forces so that the Japanese military could initiate offensive actions throughout the Pacific without opposition.

In the days that followed, the radio was on most of the time, and everyone within five miles of a radio most likely heard the broadcasts made by President Roosevelt. We listened as he focused our attention on the outrageous attack on Pearl Harbor and then asked Congress to pass a Declaration of War against Japan, Germany, and their allies. Speaking calmly in measured and formal tones, he was very persuasive, a leader who instilled confidence and a national purpose at a time when we most needed both. Supported by Congress and the nation, he galvanized the country into action with his words as he began to mobilize our industrial and military might for the challenges that would surely come.

During the early days of a war environment, something that was foreign to us, a very real fear existed that our enemies might launch another attack against us before we were ready. Intending to be prepared, soldiers dug in along California beaches while those on the East Coast got ready to fight off invaders. Unfortunately, the fears of an invasion along the West Coast prompted a decision to place in internment camps residents of Japanese ancestry. Well over one hundred thousand had to leave their homes and go to hastily built resettlement centers inland, even though seven out of ten were American citizens. In a very real sense, they were early casualties of the war, interned by fellow citizens. In Washington, D.C., tall buildings became sites for anti-aircraft guns and soldiers stood watch for enemy planes. Near the Capitol, at a secret field, the Army Air Force kept a bomber warmed up for the purpose of getting the President away from Washington in the event of an attack. In New England most of the coastline remained blacked out to avoid the possibility of presenting targets to German submarines. For many this was the most serious crisis the nation had faced since the outbreak of the Civil War. The war we were getting ready for at a leisurely pace, and hoping we'd never have to fight, came with a sudden abruptness and violence. While uncertainty and confusion created much anxiety, there began to emerge across the nation a tremendous sense of duty, a willingness to sacrifice, work together and do what was necessary to win the war. It would be a time like no other, a sharing of danger and a common purpose in a rare spirit of closeness that generations to follow would never know. The first unexpected benefit of the war would be an exceptional spirit of unity.

CHAPTER **16**

The Home Front
━━━━━━━ ◆◆◆ ━━━━━━━

Whites Crossing, Simpson and Carbondale reacted quickly to the sudden impact of the war. The response from these relatively small areas reflected precisely what was taking place in every city, hamlet, or village across the land. Those in our community eligible to serve stood ready to do whatever was necessary when called into one of the branches of the military. Many declined to wait for the draft board to call them, even though the process sharply increased when war began. Long lines crowded the recruiting stations in Scranton and Wilkes Barre, and numerous young men from the area took buses to those locations to enlist and quickly enter the service. They understood, of course, that their obligation could be for an indefinite period since there was no way to tell how long the war would last. Many tearful farewells took place at bus and train stations as scores of young men and women left for places whose names would become familiar to all of us: Fort Dix, Indiantown Gap, Great Lakes Naval Training Station, Scott Field, Bainbridge, and Parris Island. Two popular songs of the day, *I'll Be Seeing You* and *I'll Walk Alone*, captured both the mood and the reality of what was taking place on a personal basis. It was a proud time, a time of sacrifice and courage mixed with much uncertainty and a touch of sadness.

The Scranton Tribune and *The Scranton Times* faithfully reported on the coming and going of our servicemen and women, often including pictures. Train and bus stations seemed constantly filled with people in uniforms of olive drab, navy blue, and marine green. Men in uniform became a common sight in stores, churches, movie theaters and taverns in our community, symbols of the massive mobilization taking place throughout America. Everywhere we looked was evidence of a growing military might. Growing at the same time was a remarkably intense pride in every person in uniform, including those who just completed basic training and were a long way from seeing combat. It didn't matter; everyone in uniform was an instant hero to those who waited at home. Friends and neighbors warmly greeted servicemen home on furlough with wide smiles and hardy handshakes, or hugs and kisses from the ladies. It was an expression of respect, caring and gratitude for one who could be in serious danger within a few short months. It was also a reflection of enormous pride at seeing one of our own in uniform during a time of war. The mischievous boys of yesterday were suddenly young men taking on an awesome and dangerous responsibility. The circumstances brought to the surface a mixture of love and concern, emotions that might have remained mute under other conditions.

The exceptional good will toward those in uniform generated some unexpected benefits for servicemen. Drivers would stop to offer rides, even when the person in service was not hitch-hiking. A stop at one of the local taverns would result in offers to have more drinks than any reasonable person could possibly handle. Families living close to training bases invited servicemen to their homes over the holiday season to share in a family dinner at Thanksgiving or Christmas. Perhaps the largest organization devoted to easing the loneliness of servicemen far from home was the United Service Organization, USO. Staffed by civilian volunteers, USO Canteens of all sizes became established all over the country. They offered a place for traveling servicemen or those on a brief leave to relax, eat, and meet people. The larger USO Canteens arranged dances, hired bands, and invited carefully chaperoned young ladies to mingle, dance, talk and enjoy an evening with men of their own age. These brief meetings frequently resulted in a long-term wartime correspondence that led to relationships lasting a lifetime. The goodwill shown at home and in places far from home was deeply sincere and often moving. For the moment it masked the reality that many of the young men held in such esteem would soon be in extreme danger as they put into practice their specialized training in the grim tasks of war.

The intensive efforts to prepare the country for war continued at a rapid pace. The initial wartime budget, set at fifty-nine billion dollars, helped to fill the ranks with the military forces required and supply the ships, planes, tanks, and arms that would allow us to take the war to the enemy. Eventually, there would be sixteen million men and women in uniform, four times more than had served in World War I. While the nation rushed to get ready, a mixture of news came from the battlefronts. Japan won victory after victory in the Philippines, capturing many Americans and forcing General MacArthur to flee to Australia. Manila had fallen and our positions at Bataan and Corregidor were all but overwhelmed. The U.S. Navy successfully attacked the Japanese at Marshall and Gilbert Islands, but the Japanese bombed Darwin, Australia. Germany still controlled most of continental Europe and our side, in many areas, took defensive positions. There was no long series of victories in early 1942 to indicate the tides of war were turning in our favor.

Then, on April 18, 1942, a single event took place that raised the spirits of the nation immeasurably. General James Doolittle led a bombing attack on Tokyo using B-25 bombers that took off from the carrier *Hornet* after it had successfully maneuvered within flying distance of Japan. The news was sensational; we had struck a blow at the capital of our enemy and scored a meaningful victory. The psychological impact of the raid, coming less than five months after the massive destruction at Pearl Harbor, was incredible. It demonstrated an ability to strike back, brought a higher level of intensity to war preparations, and significantly raised morale. While the attack did relatively little physical damage to Tokyo, it abruptly brought the war to Japan's capital, shocked its population, and clearly demonstrated a vulnerability to attacks. It raised the fear of more bombing raids on the homeland, increased the possibility of invasion, and removed any feelings of security the Japanese might have had before Doolittle's raid. From a strategic perspective, it caused the Japanese leaders to plan for the spending of valuable war assets for defense of the home islands.

It became increasingly apparent before the end of 1942 that our government needed those on the home front in America to make sacrifices for the good of the country and its troops. The armed forces had to have first priority on all resources, a situation almost everyone respected. As a result, rationing of numerous items began. Among the very first resources to be rationed was gasoline. Actually, the rationing of gas was more to save rubber than fuel. The materials for making rubber tires were much more difficult to obtain than gasoline. In any event, depending on the use of each vehicle, automobile owners received a stamp and prominently displayed it on the windshield. An A stamp meant the vehicle use was occasional and allowed the purchase of three and one half gallons of gas per week. The B stamp was for working commuters while the last stamp, E, was for emergency vehicles, police, clergy, and farmers. There was no limit on gasoline for those holding E stamps. Our Chevrolet Victoria Coupe had the restrictive A stamp; it pleased us to have about ten gallons of gas stored in the garage before rationing became effective. A fringe benefit of gas rationing was a dramatic decline in traffic-related deaths during the war years. At least part of that decline resulted from the fact that new cars were not made during the war; the automobile industry was busy making trucks, tanks, and other vehicles for the armed forces.

Other rationed items included meat, butter, sugar, canned goods, and coffee. When we went to Fedor's store for groceries, we took along our ration booklets. The red stamps were for meat and butter while the blue stamps were for canned goods. Similar to the situation with gasoline, the rationing of canned goods was not so much because the food was in short supply but because the armed forces needed tin, much of it for the packaging of C rations for military personnel. Since each book of stamps had to last for a fixed period of time, shopping involved some careful planning. Coffee was hard to get and expensive and many families, ours included, tried to use a substitute. One such substitute, made from chicory, produced an awful-tasting brew having little resemblance to coffee. We even tried Ovaltine, a powdered mixture added to hot water. The results were slightly better but completely failed to produce the satisfaction obtained from a hot cup of coffee.

The entire nation responded to the request from national leaders to plant Victory Gardens as a way of supplying vegetables and reducing the demand for canned goods. Approximately twenty-one million families planted Victory Gardens during the war, some city folks putting in crops in the short grassy space between sidewalks and curbs. My grandfather increased the size of his large garden, and I can recall our working side by side down long rows of potatoes to remove bugs from the leaves. Along with gardening, people collected and donated scrap iron for processing and use in the making of arms. The demand for military clothing of all types resulted in clothing shortages for civilians and inspired some innovative tailoring. For men, a Victory Suit came with narrow lapels, no vest, one pair of pants without cuffs, and a short jacket. Saving material was the main objective. Even the makers of Lucky Strike cigarettes got into the war effort by abandoning the traditional green packaging with the red circle in the center. The slogan for the new white package of cigarettes was, "Lucky Strike green has gone to war." I never knew what that meant, but I suspect it was an advertising ploy. In general, while more people were working and had more money, there was less to spend it on. Still, the mood was confident and good, especially as we began to sense that the sacrifices were paying off and more victories were close at hand. In supporting those in the service, no sacrifice was too great, no effort too difficult. Those who served were not faceless and unknown; they were family, neighbors and friends, the communities' ultimate contribution to the war.

By this time Ruth had a personal link to the war through a friendship that had developed early in 1942 with a young man from Forest City, a small town about four miles northeast of Whites Crossing. Stanley Markunas was one of many sons in a Lithuanian family, his parents being among those who immigrated to that part of Pennsylvania to start a new life. He was a robust young man with tightly curled brown hair tinged with red. Friendly, open, and outgoing, he had a genuine fondness for people and was always ready for a good time. He was also an exceptionally energetic polka dancer. Early on, it became obvious he had a serious interest in Ruth, a fact that did not bring joy to his parents. They, like many other parents then, would have preferred that he dated his "own kind," and Ruth was half-Irish. This initial reaction would undergo a dramatic turnaround once they learned to know Ruth.

Stanley became a member of the United States Army in mid-1942 and, after basic training, drew an assignment to the Signal Corps. His specialized training was in providing communications under battlefield conditions and at command posts. Before the end of 1942 his unit sailed to England, and it would be three years before he would return to the United States. Remarkably, he and Ruth kept their relationship intact over the three year period by exchanging a long series of letters, often using V-Mail, a light, one-page document that, when folded, contained a preprinted section on the reverse side for an address. They exchanged pictures and gifts, and despite the long, lonely separation, their friendship and affection, like that of other young couples in similar situations, remained strong and promising.

While we adapted to the numerous changes taking place in our lives, many of the country's leaders became convinced that the possibility of air attacks, especially along the East and West Coasts, remained very real. It was not uncommon for people on the East Coast to stand near the shore of the Atlantic Ocean and watch the glow on the horizon caused by burning ships, ships destroyed by the German submarine fleet. Attacks that close and visible from land fueled the suggestion that bombing of eastern cities was not unlikely. For that as well as other reasons, an organization called Civil Defense became an important part of our lives. A primary responsibility of Civil Defense was to conduct blackouts and air raid drills. When the air raid sirens sounded, the first response of the people in the community was to turn out all the lights in and around every house. The objective was to avoid providing illuminated targets or landmarks for enemy bombers. With my mother and Pat working in Newton, New Jersey, during many of the early drills, Ruth and I took the responsibility very seriously, especially since there was always a small chance the air raid was for real. We played the radio during the drills in the event that emergency broadcasts provided air raid reports or special instructions. However, I always put a towel over the radio to hide the glow from the dial. While seeing such a light from thousands of feet in the air was virtually impossible, we wanted to avoid any possibility of inadvertently helping the enemy. Our house completely darkened, I hurried to various windows to see how quickly the neighbors were getting blacked out. The response time was usually quite good, and when it was not, I would do more than a little seething.

A complete blackout produced an unusual atmosphere. Everything, it seemed, came to a stop. Our world was totally dark, very still and quite eerie, as if the entire population had paused in the midst of their activities and strained to hear the sound of approaching planes. From the darkness of our home we would watch as air raid wardens passed by each house on the street, ensuring a complete blackout in the neighborhood. In the background the radio would be playing softly and many air raid drills at our home were conducted to the music of Harry James, Sammy Kaye, Glenn Miller, and especially Tommy Dorsey; his band featured a young, skinny singing sensation named Frank Sinatra. In about thirty minutes the all-clear sirens signaled an end to the blackout and air raid drill. For the brief time that each lasted, it seemed we had an emotional link with the war, a special feeling that in a small way we were playing a part in this great conflict. Perhaps that's why we always wanted a perfect drill every time.

CHAPTER 17

Visit From a War Plane

♦♦♦

While working in Newton, Pat received notification of his induction into the armed services. The normal series of mental and physical tests found him fit for duty, and his orders directed him to report to the Army post at Fort Dix, New Jersey, on February 3, 1943. As a family we now had a direct connection to the war, a situation that generated both pride and apprehension. The circumstances of the past few years had made us a very close-knit family and it seemed strange to see the group reduced by one, especially the oldest of the children. This had a particular impact on my mother; she had great concerns about the dangers posed by a war that appeared to be consuming the entire world and showed no sign of ending in the near future. Pat's leaving also came at a time when she was starting to feel reasonably comfortable. The family had two steady income sources, she and Pat worked at the same place and lived in the same rooming house, and Ruth continued her exceptional work in maintaining the homestead at Whites Crossing and caring for Gene. Deep down, she may have sensed that Pat's going into the service marked the first of many new changes to come and, ready or not, she would have to accommodate them.

Getting letters and cards from Pat was a new experience, especially with the word "Free" written in the corner where the stamp was usually placed. The mail immediately became a way to track his progress and, at the same time, get a small view into army life. From Fort Dix he went to Miami Beach for basic training, a fact that was astounding to those of us who had never traveled more than two hours from home. At Miami Beach Pat was found to have the aptitude to be a Radio Operator and Mechanic. This resulted in his being sent to Scott Field in Illinois for training and assignment to the Army Air Force. Following this tour of duty, he went to Philadelphia for advanced radio training at the Philco Training Center and later reported to the Army Air Force Technical School located at Truax Field, Madison, Wisconsin. With much of the technical training behind him, Pat's next assignment took him to the Smoky Hill Army Air Base near Salina, Kansas, to apply what he had learned to the serious business of flying.

Initial training on B-26 medium bombers, regarded as highly dangerous planes, impressed on him immediately that wartime flying was going to be a very risky business. Fortunately, training emphasis soon switched to the B-17 Flying Fortress, a plane that was much more reliable and stable. Training on the B-17, and later the B-29 Super Fortress, consisted of long-range simulated bombing missions, both day and night, on cities all over the United States. In the letters we received, it was clear the training could be grueling and repetitive, a constant striving to get all aspects right before flying missions in hostile territory. At the same time, it was apparent that Pat found the special camaraderie that develops among a crew dependent upon each other for survival and success a new and satisfying experience. They trained hard, partied well, and in the process forged a unity that was akin to brotherhood.

The few times Pat was able to get home on furlough were warm and pleasant for the entire clan and made my mother beam with

Pat Rowland and Mother Mary

pride. It was obvious he had grown in maturity, liked his military assignment, and had unlimited confidence in his fellow airmen and in flying. The stripes on his uniform were evidence of success in his job while the Air Force patch on his left shoulder and the silver wings on his uniform were symbols that made each of us very proud. He represented all of us in this great war, and our pleasure in his accomplishments was beyond measure. Some of his most conspicuous personality traits seemed magnified by military service. His gregarious, fun-loving nature—much like that of our father—was at a higher level and added to the joy of those eager to welcome him home. In one respect he did not change, and that was in the continuation of his courtship of Helen Erzin. It was obvious that, for them, the occasional furloughs were brief points of happiness separated by extended periods of intense loneliness. They made the most of their limited time together; our family Chevrolet stood parked outside the Erzin homestead every furlough evening, a situation we all understood.

While Pat continued his training throughout 1943, the war raged on in Europe, Africa, and the Pacific. Victories that began to mount up for our side did not come easily or without great sacrifice. In the Pacific the Marines took Guadalcanal from the Japanese after six months of intense fighting and thousands of casualties on both sides. This unrelenting, protracted battle would appear, in retrospect, as a learning experience in how to invade islands and fight an enemy who preferred death to surrender. The Russians, having won a decisive battle at Stalingrad early in the year, continued to demonstrate that the tide may have turned against Germany on the Eastern front. Land recently won by Germany at tremendous costs fell to the advancing Russian Army. The Desert Fox of the German Army, General Rommel, suffered a major defeat in North Africa and returned to Germany to face a future that was uncertain at best. The United States invaded Sicily in July 1943, a move that hastened the removal of the dictator, Mussolini, from office. In October 1943, the attack on the "soft underbelly of Europe" continued when the allies launched the invasion of Italy. With the appointment of General Eisenhower to Supreme Allied Commander on December 1, 1943, speculation began about a possible invasion of France. Newspaper accounts of local casualties considerably tempered the good news coming from various battlefronts. Early in the war many of those being wounded or killed seemed to be from somewhere else. It was a bit easier to be happily belligerent about the favorable course of the war when unknown people were paying the price. Now, the war was coming home in a way we had not planned.

In the early 1940s there were few in our area who had had any experience of flying, even as passengers. None of our relatives and no one in our immediate family had ever flown before Pat entered the Army Air Force. For the most part, the only large planes we saw were in newsreels and movies. Of course, we were familiar with Charles Lindbergh, Amelia Earhart and the World War I flying ace, Eddie Rickenbacker, but as a group we were totally unsophisticated when it came to flying. My grandparents were even more naive than the rest of us on such matters; they were content to remain forever earthbound. On one of Pat's furloughs, as we stood in the basement kitchen at their home and visited, he talked about the B-17 Flying Fortress and his enthusiasm for a new bomber, the B-29 Super Fortress. All of us had trouble comprehending the size of the planes, and our grandparents were having more serious problems understanding how high the planes could fly. Pat was not allowed to discuss the flying capabilities of the planes, the B-29 in particular, but I guessed it might fly as high as least six miles. As he explained the flying altitude to our grandparents in terms of land mile distance, it was apparent such a thing was a wonder that they could hardly believe. Picturing Pat in a plane that high above the earth was quite unsettling for both of them. My grandmother's reaction was to call for divine intervention to protect Pat and his crew while my grandfather covered his concern with a scowl. At the time, none of us expected to see a Flying Fortress up close, flying right above our neighborhood.

On a warm day in September 1943, many of our neighbors were outdoors in the late afternoon when the low rumble of a very large plane attracted our attention. It was coming in our direction, passing over a mountain directly north of Simpson and flying at a low altitude. We moved quickly to the small hill at the rear of our lot for a better view. The sight of the huge, four-engine Flying Fortress coming toward us at such a low level was absolutely stunning. Instantly, everyone came to the same conclusion: Pat and his crew were on the plane. We began shouting, waving frantically, and running toward more open areas, trying hard to send the message that we saw them and hoped they saw us. As the plane passed overhead, the roar of the engines drowned out all other sound and seemed to vibrate the earth, but still we shouted and waved. When it stayed on a course directly over New Dam, we were certain the dam had served as a land-mark to line up the pass over the neighborhood. As the plane moved into the distance, the excitement was slow to subside. We all tried to explain, all at the same time, what we had seen. On one point we all agreed: anything that big and magnificent would surely win the war for us. As we stood there talking excitedly, we suddenly realized the plane, still very low, was returning, coming in now from the east for a pass over Simpson. This pass, we realized, was for Helen, and that inspired a fresh round of smiles and cheers. We watched as the plane passed over Simpson, climbed and swung in a great arc to the east, and disappeared from view. We sensed it would not be back, but still we waited, reluctant to leave after an event that had filled us with so much pride and emotion. Those feelings stayed with us for a very long time.

Somewhere in the country the practice began of putting small pennants in the front windows of homes to tell all who passed by that someone in that family was serving, or had served, in the armed forces. Usually, families displayed one pennant for each member in the military. Although there was some variation in the design, most were about twelve inches in length and eight inches wide. Sewn into the top was a quarter-inch piece of rounded wood. This provided stability to the pennant as well as anchor points for braided, gold-colored cord used to hang the pennant to the inside of the window. A two-inch red border surrounded a white rectangular center, and the side and bottom edges of the pennant had a gold-colored fringe. Imprinted inside the white rectangular center was a star, either in blue or gold. The blue star proudly signified that a member of the household was in the service. A gold star delivered the poignant message that the person being honored had been killed in action or had died from wounds.

Noticing pennants soon became instinctive for most people. Unconsciously, I think, we wanted to look and see only blue stars, a symbol that served as a bond between all those who had someone at risk. A gold star, even at the home of people unknown, caused sharp, sudden sorrow and left a lingering, uneasy reminder that we were all vulnerable to a similar loss. It is unlikely that I ever missed seeing each pennant displayed along the way to Carbondale or other places, and the color of each star was first to catch my attention. Perhaps I needed some assurance that the blue stars far exceeded the gold. The pennant at our house was in the parlor window, just to the left of the front door. Clearly visible from the road, it sent the message that, for the moment at least, all was well. Inevitably, losses occurred, and when they came, sorrow swept like a depressing gray fog over the entire community.

A loss takes on greater significance when there is some acquaintance, however casual. We became familiar with two brothers of Italian descent simply because they operated a shoe repair business in a small shop across from Saint Rose Church in Carbondale. When the shop closed for the duration of the war, we understood the situation and looked forward to it being reopened when the brothers returned from service. In this case it was not to be. Within the span of a few months after going overseas, both died in action. As a community, we never anticipated one family losing two sons, and in this extraordinary loss we all assumed a share of the two gold stars and the pain that came with them.

In mid-1943 we learned of plans to build a memorial to honor the servicemen and women from Whites Crossing. That fine idea

Memorial at Whites Crossing

appealed to me immensely. Many towns and villages in the area were honoring their own, and it seemed absolutely right that we should do the same. That summer, however, I joined some of my friends in going to work at Lake Minnewaska, an elegant old resort in the Catskill Mountains of New York. As a result, I was not present to watch the work progress on this important community project. During my months at Lake Minnewaska I often thought about the memorial, especially when I followed the war news in the *New York Daily News*, and I looked forward to seeing it. As soon as I returned home to stay, in early September, I walked to Whites Crossing to see the finished memorial.

Selecting a better location for the memorial did not seem possible. It stood where the road through Whites Crossing branched left and right. Sitting on land owned by the Costolnick family, it was at the village crossroads and in plain view of all those coming through the center of Whites Crossing. Carefully crafted from wood and mounted on two four-inch posts, the memorial's red and blue trim highlighted the basic white background. The names of those being honored, printed in black on name plates mounted with precision to the memorial, stood out sharply against the fresh white paint. The memorial had a simple beauty about it that was moving to behold. It was evident that this was a work inspired by love and caring, a proud tribute of a community to its sons and daughters. At least twice I read each of the original sixty-three names on the memorial, recognizing almost all of them and noting the blank spaces remaining for names to be added. Even as I absorbed the beauty and meaning of this deeply personal memorial, the realization that it was so impermanent filled me with regret. The memorial, in my idealistic young mind, should have been made of granite, the names chiseled deep into that hard stone to serve as an enduring reminder to generations to come that from this small village an extraordinary number of young people responded to the call to arms and served with great bravery, honor and distinction. Among them was an airman whose wartime actions resulted in his being awarded the Congressional Medal of Honor, posthumously.

In April 1944, Pat's squadron of B-29 bombers left the Smoky Hill Air Base for combat duty. After landing in Maine to refuel, they continued on to Gander Air Base in Newfoundland for a two-day stay. The temperature at that base was twelve degrees below zero. With the squadron flying in formation to their next destination, Casablanca, the plane on which Pat and his crew

Crew of the *Mary K*
Pat Rowland—front row, second from right

were flying developed engine trouble over the North Atlantic, three hours after leaving Newfoundland. Forced to turn back, the plane limped back to Gander Air Base. Since the mechanics specializing in B-29 maintenance, along with most spare parts, were headed by ship to the final destination point, the crew assumed the responsibility for repairing the plane. It took eight days and thirty-six borrowed spark plugs to return the plane's engines to normal operation. The fact that there was so much water to cross before reaching North Africa provided a strong motivation for quality repairs. Although the plane was now now ready to fly, a spring thaw caused the runways to soften and become unsafe for the heavy B-29 bomber to use for take-off. It would be three more weeks before the runways became solid enough to permit a take-off.

To the relief of the entire crew, the flight to Casablanca was uneventful. It was a bit strange, however, not to be in formation with other planes from the squadron. After a brief stop at Casablanca, the crew continued on to Cairo, flying over the battlefields where the German Desert Fox, General Rommel, saw early victories and ultimate defeat. Two days at Cairo allowed for a quick trip to the Pyramids while maintenance crews serviced the plane. The next stop and final destination was in India, at a base ninety miles north of Calcutta. The United States took the original base, which Germany had occupied during World War I, expanded the size, and converted it into an airfield for both B-29 bombers and fighter planes. Japanese positions all over Southeast Asia bore the brunt of attacks by B-29 bombers initiating missions from this base. All missions would be long and harrowing, some beginning with a flight over the Himalayan mountains to an advance base in China, from which certain raids took place. Other bombing attacks involved exceptionally hours of flight from the home base in India to the targets and return. The training of the crew, intensely developed over the previous year, was now at its highest level and ready for the ultimate test. The major objectives of successfully completing each mission and returning safely to base would bring from each member a total commitment in skill and energy every time the plane left the ground. From such circumstances are forged the bonds that make a crew a family.

CHAPTER **18**

Last One in Line

◆◆◆

In early 1944 it became apparent that our side was growing in strength and the tides of war were turning in our favor. By late January German forces were all but driven from Russian soil. The campaign that Hitler anticipated would be swift, overwhelming, and complete had turned into a major German disaster. His forces had suffered a major defeat in North Africa and now Italy was about to fall to the allies. At the same time, the mobilization of allied troops in Great Britain strongly suggested an invasion of France was imminent. In the Far East, General MacArthur began a drive through the Pacific, by-passing some islands held by the Japanese and invading those of more strategic value. Japan began calling up students for military service, a sign that losses were high and invasions of the homeland feared. In April 1944, United States planes bombed Berlin for the first time, using B-17 bombers in a daylight raid. By the end of May it was becoming clear that the United States and Great Britain had established air superiority over Germany. The massive production of arms in the United

States, for ourselves and our allies, and the intensive mobilization of American troops was making a major difference in the course of the war. And, although the Axis forces were far from defeated, they were on the defensive in many areas.

As actions on the battlefields continued at an unrelenting pace, the combination of enlistments and the draft saw more and more of my neighborhood friends going to the train station to report for duty in one of the branches of the service. Following basic training, they usually came home in uniform for a brief furlough before moving on to the next assignment. Looking older, trim and sharp in uniform, I envied them greatly, and regretted that I was the youngest boy in my close circle of friends. Age difference had not been much of a factor in the past, but suddenly I was too young to join the military and too old, at least in my mind, to be staying home with the older men, women and children. It was a major frustration. I had followed the war with an intense interest for a long time, and all that I read, saw in newsreels, and heard on the radio convinced me that it was the greatest battle for good in the history of man. It was, I felt, the most momentous happening of a lifetime, something I wanted to share with the many already involved in making history. All around me and throughout the country, "ordinary people were doing extraordinary things" while I watched my peers leave one at a time and followed the war's progress, both successes and failures, in newspapers. I had strongly ambivalent feelings. I prayed for the war to end and for the safe return of our troops while fervently wishing I would be a part of this great conflict before it was over.

June 1944 was a month filled with dramatic war activity. Allied troops entered Rome and B-29 bombers struck Tokyo, the first attack on the city since General Doolittle's raid in 1942. During the same month, American forces invaded the island of Saipan. Its ultimate capture resulted in an air base for B-29 bombers being established much closer to Japan. Of equal if not greater importance, it also provided a landing site for damaged bombers from other bases, bombers that otherwise would have come down in the ocean. The victory at Saipan was responsible for saving hundreds of airmen and aircraft while bringing the war a giant step closer to the Japanese homeland. On June 6, 1944, the long expected invasion of France began, launched by the greatest armada of ships ever assembled for such a purpose. The scope and fury of the assault by allied forces at Normandy electrified the world. But concern about the outcome of this tremendously complex undertaking tempered our elation. Within days the code names used for the beaches where troop landings took place, Utah, Omaha, Gold, Juno and Sword, would become known in every household. The nation figuratively held its breath as we waited to see if the Germans might repel the invasion forces. When the Allies captured thirty thousand German troops at Cherbourg and the advance into Normandy grew broader and deeper, we began to feel more confident. In August Paris was liberated, an emotional event that marked both the freeing of a captive people and the extraordinary success of the allied forces. While victories mounted and were a cause for elation, there was always the awareness that success on the battlefields came at a very high price.

While I was waiting for my turn in the military, many of those who shared my boyhood were serving the country, and some were continually at risk. Pat's missions to bomb targets all over Southeast Asia were a constant source of concern, especially because the flying time was so extensive and increasing numbers of Japanese kamikaze pilots, intent on sacrificing their lives to bring down the huge B-29 bombers, posed a deadly threat. Teddy Falong, a friend whose family lived just two doors from our home, served in the Army and took part in the bloody fighting that raged in the mountains of Italy, an exceptionally excruciating experience. Eddie Calafut served with the Marines, moving from one Pacific island to the next, doing his job under difficult and dangerous circumstances. His brother, Johnny, was a member of the U.S. Army, as were my next-door cousins, Johnny and Mike Klickus. From the family on the other side of our home, Edmund Zukowski was serving in the Army while his brother, Chet, was in the Navy. From this cluster of only five neighborhood homes came eight servicemen, all part of our close community family, absent friends now represented by blue stars in the window. I wanted very much to be a part of that group.

I made a promising, hopeful step toward active service when I became a member of the Air Corps Enlisted Reserve. In July of 1944, after I turned seventeen, I applied for admission into the Army Air Cadet program. The program provided an opportunity to qualified enlistees to train for flying positions in the Army Air Force. The most qualified in the Air Cadet program might become pilots, navigators, or bombardiers while others could qualify for different flying positions. Becoming an Air Cadet involved extensive physical and mental testing, a process that continually left me in doubt about my being selected for the program. The letter notifying me of my acceptance still ranks as one of the most gratifying pieces of mail I ever received. On August 23, 1944, I joined other enlistees at a recruiting office in Wilkes-Barre for a swearing-in ceremony. Along with a packet of documents, I received a small emblem of golden wings with the circled initials AC directly in the center. It was an emblem I treasured greatly. The bus trip back to Carbondale passed quickly and I smiled all the way home. I left Wilkes-Barre with the understanding that a call to active service would come in early 1945. The date seemed a long way off in the future. Still, I was getting closer to doing my part in the war, and going into the Army Air Force added special meaning to what was taking place. Being in the same branch of service as Pat really appealed to me. I'd been following his lead for a long time and, after hearing his accounts of flying, reading his letters, and seeing a B-17 bomber at close range, it seemed like the natural thing to do.

I was the sole remaining member of my peer group still on the home front waiting for my turn. I was the last one in line. This had been so since April 1944, when my old friend Chet Zukowski joined the U.S. Navy and left for basic training at Bainbridge, Maryland. Chet had been my next door neighbor. He was about one year older than I, and we became the best of friends at a very early age. We skated and went sledding together, fished where we shouldn't have, picked blueberries in the mountains, and worked mightily on the swimming hole with our neighborhood buddies. As a young boy, I spent more than a few mornings having a breakfast of buttered homemade bread and coffee in the Zukowski kitchen before we went off to do something. When the opportunity came to spend a summer working at the Lake Minnewaska resort in the Catskill Mountains of New York, Chet was quick to urge me to go with him. Later, before we were of legal age to do so, we would sample our first beer together in a Simpson tavern and instantly learn that smoking a first White Owl cigar at the same time was not a good idea.

By September 1944, Chet was a crew member on the U.S.S. *Quincy*, a heavy cruiser that would soon take part in an historic mission. On January 23, 1945, at Newport News, the ship picked up President Roosevelt, his daughter, Anna, and presidential advisors. The mission was to deliver the President and his party safely to what would become known as the Yalta Conference. Arriving at the isle of Malta on February 2, the President was joined by Prime Minister Winston Churchill and the U.S. Ambassador to Russia, Averill Harriman. The ship later docked in Egypt where the leaders left for Yalta to confer with Premier Joseph Stalin. The President returned to the U.S.S. *Quincy* on February 12 and, under the same heavy escort of planes, aircraft carriers, and other ships that had ensured his safe passage to Egypt, returned to Newport News by the end of the month. Following this extraordinary assignment, the U.S.S. *Quincy* would leave for the Pacific by way of the Panama Canal and Pearl Harbor to take part in the battle for Okinawa. The war experiences of my friend contrasted sharply with my inaction as a reservist.

> Late in 1944 President Roosevelt and Prime Minister Winston Churchill agreed to focus more attention on the war in the Pacific. The meeting at Yalta in February 1945 confirmed that strategy and included plans to intensify the war against the Japanese. As it turned out, even before new strategies began, some significant events were taking place in the Pacific. Americans liberated Manila and invaded the island of Iwo Jima, an action that would produce the most famous photograph of the war, the raising of the American flag on top of Mount Surabachi. This magnificent action photo captured with simple eloquence the moment of an heroic victory and the spirit, determination and sacrifice of American troops. For the entire nation it symbolized that coming together in a common cause was resulting in the attainment of a common goal: victory. By the end of February 1945, carrier planes were attacking military installations on the outskirts of Tokyo while squadrons of B-29 bombers were bombing the city. We had learned through harsh

experience, however, that the Japanese were a tenacious foe, prepared to fiercely contest every foot of land they regarded as their own. There were no illusions about quick, easy victories.

On April 12, 1945, the United States suffered a major loss when President Roosevelt died suddenly while resting from the rigors of war at a retreat in Warm Springs, Georgia. Elected to four consecutive terms as President, he had proved to be a strong, talented leader, one who began his presidency intent on leading the nation out of the greatest economic depression the country had ever known. At war, his stature as President reached new heights as he rallied the people of the nation into action and encouraged them to act as one in the cause of freedom. Though handicapped early in life by polio, he was unsparing of his time and energy. Taking a very active part in all phases of the war, he held numerous meetings with allied leaders, directed the planning of military strategy, and conducted the mobilization and arming of the nation. His was a familiar and frequent voice on the radio; reassuring, instilling confidence, and bringing a sense of national purpose to a country at war. The physical toll became increasingly apparent as the war years passed; by 1945 he looked much older, worn and tired. In pictures taken at the Yalta Conference he appeared almost frail. The nation not only lost a leader; it also lost a father figure, a man who had led the nation for more than a decade. The national mourning for the President was intense. The leader of the Republican opposition in the Congress, Senator Robert Taft, said of Roosevelt in a speech before his colleagues, "He was a hero of the war for he literally worked himself to death for the American people." There was universal regret that the President would not see the final results of his exceptional leadership and gifted labors since he had given so much of himself for so long.

On the same day that the President died, a shocked and humbled Vice President, Harry S Truman, took the oath of office for President, vowing to complete the work President Roosevelt had carried to a magnificent level. After a seemingly slow start in that great office, the new President would reveal himself to be feisty, decisive, and courageous. Before the war would end he would rank as an equal of other world leaders and make decisions that would give him a unique place in the history of both the country and the world.

CHAPTER **19**

Coming Home

━━━━━━━━━━ ◆◆◆ ━━━━━━━━━━

In the fall of 1944, my mother succeeded in finding employment at a textile mill in Scranton, a job that ended four years of working in Newton, New Jersey, and rushing home each Friday night to look after her family. While we had functioned well in her absence and had gotten used to the responsibility, having her home again full-time was comparable to receiving an unexpected but warmly welcomed gift. It was also good to share Pat's letters with her on the very day they arrived. Since the letters were subject to review by military censors, we often tried to get from them more than was actually written. While I am sure our guesses about what might be happening with Pat's bomber group were often wrong, we were keenly aware the situation they were in was stressful and dangerous. That became evident one day when a letter containing a few pictures arrived from India. I was the only one at home at the time, and when I opened the letter and looked at the pictures, I was soon wishing my mother or Ruth was there to confirm what I saw. One of the photographs stunned me. It showed an unsmiling, weary and somber Pat, totally unlike his usual self. His face looked thin and gaunt, and dark circles highlighted eyes that seemed to project an infinite sadness. It appeared the combination of long, tension-filled flights to bomb distant targets, kamikaze attacks, lost friends and planes, and the relentless heat of India was taking an alarming toll.

Eager to get another opinion of the picture, I hurried to my grandparents' home hoping to find my mother or Ruth. They were not there, so I decided to get my grandparents' reaction. Acting as nonchalantly as I could manage, I told them about the letter, handed the pictures to my grandmother, and instantly realized it was not the right thing to do. My grandmother shed tears easily, even when she was happy. I might have discounted her reaction had not my normally calm, stoical grandfather, after studying that particular picture for a long time, appeared deeply moved. Handing the picture to me, he commented in his distinctive broken English about the bad things that war does to people and walked outdoors to deal with his thoughts in his own way. By the time I returned the short distance to our home, my perspective on the war had changed. This war was suddenly much closer to our family; one of our own was not only at serious risk, but the war also extracted a huge price even when the participants managed to stay alive. The glamour of war, seen best by those at great distance from the conflict, suddenly diminished. I realized that, when standing on the sidelines while others are winning battles, we tend to focus on the heroics and glory that reflects well on all of us, forgetting, for the moment at least, the countless personal sacrifices, both large and small, that make each victory possible.

As I waited for the call to active duty in the Army Air Force, I learned that the taxi company in Carbondale was in dire need of drivers. It appeared to be the perfect short-term job. That they would even consider a relatively new driver was a good indication that experienced help was scarce because of the war. Perhaps another reason the job remained unfilled was that the hours were from six o'clock in the evening until six the following morning. On a schedule that rotated each week, drivers received one day off. Looking at my license, the night manager noted I did not have much experience. He also learned that I qualified to drive in a 1937 Buick Roadmaster, a car with the shift stick on the floor. After some hesitation, and likely prompted by desperation, he hired me to begin work immediately. Within minutes the manager gave me my first assignment and told me which car to use. The taxi station was at the northeast corner of Main Street and Salem Avenue in Carbondale. Much of the first floor of the building was open on two sides and served as a parking area for the fleet of taxis. I walked out, noted the car was an Oldsmobile, and got into the driver's seat. The lack of a clutch or shift lever on the floor caught me by surprise. It had what was called a Hydra-matic shifting system, something I was looking at for the first time.

Feeling alarmed and a bit foolish, I studied the lever mounted near the steering wheel and the gear markings, trying to quickly figure out how to operate the car. In a short time the manager came out to find out why I was taking so long to get started. I told him, quite truthfully, that I was getting familiar with the car, but I did not say I had never driven one like it. Satisfied, he went back to his office. Putting the car in neutral and turning the key, I started the car. Holding the foot brake firmly, I shifted to what I took to be reverse, eased up on the brake and felt greatly relieved when the car backed away from the wall. Gaining more confidence, I put the car in drive and was on my way. While it turned out to be easy, it was a long time before I stopped trying to put my left foot on a clutch pedal that was not there.

The job turned out to be a nightly adventure. Business was brisk, the people were interesting, and the tips were very good. At the time, my mother was working a shift at the textile mill in Scranton that ended at eleven o'clock in the evening. This meant she was home by midnight, which was my lunch break. I would stop at home as close to midnight as the last trip allowed, and together we would eat leftovers and drink hot tea while we counted my tips. On a good night I would have as much as ten dollars, an amount that happily amazed both of us. The irony of making that much money from driving a car for six hours was exceptionally funny. Not long ago four of us had worked much harder for much less and barely managed to get by. Those midnight luncheons were quietly pleasant, a time to talk while the rest of our world was dark and quiet. We'd talk about Pat and his latest letter and wonder when he would be coming home. Ruth's friend, Stanley, was also on our minds because he was a part of the invasion force sweeping through France. We would talk about Gene, his school work, and how tall he was growing. Our conversations covered many subjects, most dealing with the everyday business of living, but the war was always a central part of them.

The invasion of continental Europe that began as a foothold on the beaches of Normandy spread in ever-widening patterns. The German army fought with increasing desperation, resorting, in September 1944, to the call up of teenagers and old men to fill depleted ranks. Still, they continued to give up much of their conquered territory. Their last attempt to launch a major counterattack occurred in December 1944, with the Battle of the Bulge. The sudden success of this offensive in the snow-filled forests of Belgium caught the Allies by surprise. When our soldiers finally halted the drive and drove the German army back, we rejoiced in the successful defense and sensed it was Hitler's last frantic effort for victory. In a matter of months, the Germans would be fighting unsuccessfully to keep their homeland free from invading forces.

Almost unconsciously I began to think of my military service in terms of fighting against the Japanese. It appeared increasingly likely that the war in Europe would end before the Army Air Force called me to active duty. It didn't matter; defeating Hitler and his German forces as quickly as possible was something much of the world had struggled to bring about for about six years. It would bring the greatest victory for freedom and liberty the world had ever known. While we waited for the explosion of joy, relief and tears that would come with the end of the European war, I anticipated that the war in the Pacific was far from over. It seemed the character of the Japanese would not permit surrender and a fanatical defense of each island making up that nation would take place. What I did not anticipate was that the allied leaders, already thinking of Germany as a defeated enemy, were planning a major shift of experienced combat forces to the Pacific. That, I was soon to learn, would have a serious impact on my plans.

Late in February 1945 I received notice of the Army's intent to discontinue the Air Cadet program due to a surplus of trained personnel. The options open to me were to remain committed to serving in the Army Air Force in some unknown capacity, select another branch of the U.S. Army, or take a discharge. I had been expecting the letter to be a call to active duty and was devastated when I read the contents. What had appeared to be a sound foundation for a tour of duty in a branch of service I really favored had suddenly collapsed. A hurried visit to the recruiting office in Wilkes-Barre gained me a bit of sympathy but not much else. Thoroughly discouraged by this turn of events, I elected to take the discharge, thinking I might find a training program similar to the Army's in other branches of the military. However, it would take at least two months to get my discharge and pursue other alternatives. It was not a good February.

Shortly after I turned sixteen, I began to date on an occasional basis. It was new, exciting, enjoyable, and I tended to put the sweet-smelling young ladies on a pedestal; the stories I'd read about the knights of England and the age of chivalry still influenced me. However, dating was a complex issue. We still did not have a phone and making contact after meeting a girl was awkward, especially when it involved using a phone at a neighbor's home, in their presence. More than anything else, the lack of transportation limited frequent dating, especially when we lived a mile and a half from the center of Carbondale, the location of movie theaters, restaurants, and ice cream parlors. Once, I invited a girl from Whites Crossing to attend a movie with me. She was a very attractive blonde, but the experience of walking from Whites Crossing to Carbondale and back again, which involved passing my watching, smiling friends, limited our relationship to one date. Going to a dance at the social hall next to the Slovak Church was a bit easier. The bands, especially that of trumpet-playing Jimmy Juliano and his group, drew large crowds. Most often, my friends and I went to the dance without a date, and for the early part of the evening the boys stayed together and watched the girls while the girls watched back. Eventually, I would find the courage to ask a girl to dance, and we would often dance together for most of the evening. By the time the band played the final tune, usually *Good Night, Ladies*, we both understood that I would walk her home, an event that made a fine ending to some very pleasant evenings.

In the early part of 1945, I began dating a girl who lived in Carbondale, near the top of Salem Avenue, at the very edge of the city. She was petite, honey-blonde with blue eyes and I felt very flattered when it appeared she was really fond of me. Going to see her, however, was a significant challenge. It required a long walk down Canaan Street and then an equally long, but steeper walk up Salem Avenue. One evening early in May, I received an invitation to visit her at her home to play records, enjoy some snacks, and talk. It sounded like a fine idea; my spirits were low, the discharge from the Air Corps Reserve had not yet arrived and, while there was some indication Pat might be returning to the States, we were not at all sure when that would happen. Her parents greeted me cordially and then went to another part of the house while we played some favorite records and tried dancing in the living room. I'd been there for just over an hour when the phone rang. It was my sister, Ruth, calling from the home of

Staff Sergeant Pat Rowland

our neighbors, the McDonalds. When she told me Pat was home, the announcement was as unexpected as it was electrifying, but I assumed she meant he was somewhere in the United States. But no, she made it absolutely clear he was at our home.

Hanging up the phone, I told my new friend I had to leave and explained why. Disappointed, she tried hard to persuade me to stay while I could hardly restrain myself from charging out the door. I left quickly and soon began to run down Salem Avenue.

The running seemed to release both the apprehension that I had kept under control for so long and the exuberant joy of knowing Pat was really home. I laughed as I raced along, leaping over curbs and occasionally shouting with happiness. With Pat returning safely home from his overseas tour, I felt our family had won a personal part of the war and I was celebrating spontaneously and loudly. Near the lower end of Salem Avenue I turned right on Terrace Street and continued running until I crossed the small pedestrian bridge over Rachetbrook Creek at the foot of Canaan Street. Too out of breath to jog even slowly up Canaan Street, I walked briskly uphill. Canaan Street on that particular night seemed much longer than I remembered it to be.

Passing my grandparents' house, I could see lights were on throughout our home, including the front porch. At least two cars were parked in our driveway and another across the road from the house. As I approached the front yard, there was a sense of vibrant joy in the air and many happy sounds coming from inside. Bounding up the steps of the front porch, I hurried inside to join in the long-awaited celebration. There were many exceptionally cheerful people scattered throughout the house, most of them family, and in the middle of our sitting room stood Pat. In uniform, except for his jacket, he looked thin, fit and very happy. Our smiles were huge as we approached each other, vigorously shook hands and shared a brief hug. There was no need to say anything about the meaning of this moment. He knew, and so did I.

Returning home on May 1, 1945, for a thirty-day furlough, Pat's orders required him to report to the Santa Ana Air Base in California at the end of his leave. The long separation he and Helen endured, as well as the fact it was about to happen again, prompted them to talk seriously about getting married. The plan was for Helen to accompany Pat to California and stay with him until his next assignment, most likely overseas. With the help of both families and many friends, the plans for holding a wedding on short notice moved along briskly and it took place at the Slovak church in Simpson on May 26. It was an especially happy occasion because it celebrated both the marriage and Pat's safe return home. The high spirits and warm feelings made for an unusually festive reception in the social hall next to the church. Being a very pleased member of the wedding party, I did not miss any opportunities to enjoy this day and all it stood for.

Helen and Pat traveled to California by train and, upon reporting to the Santa Ana Air Base, Pat received an additional thirty-day leave for rest and recreation. Given quarters for married service personnel at a plush hotel in Santa Monica, he and Helen enjoyed thirty days of an unexpected honeymoon. Following the extended leave, Pat received orders to report to Fort Dix, New Jersey. Feeling certain this could lead to an overseas assignment in a matter of days, Helen returned home while Pat continued on to Fort Dix. After waiting for three weeks for new orders, the Army Air Force decided it had enough experienced personnel to conclude the war against Japan and began to discharge those who had served in combat. The war in Europe had ended on May 8, 1945, and this allowed for additional troops and materials being sent to the Pacific. In addition, the Japanese homeland was the target of massive bombing attacks. The general feeling among the nation's leaders was that the war might end before the New Year. The Army Air Force, however, attempted to retain those who agreed to reenlist and made efforts to persuade Pat to extend his service in this way. Feeling he had seen enough of combat flying during his year in India, he elected to return home to his new wife. On June 30, 1945, with the receipt of his discharge, he ended a period of wartime service that was intensive, dangerous and distinguished.

CHAPTER 20

The *Mary K* and Crew

◆◆◆

*I*n bits and pieces, over a long period of time, we would gain some insight into the experiences of a B-29 bomber squadron flying out of India. Pat was his usual self in all respects but one; talking about the war and combat experience made him a bit angry. The anger appeared to be the result of having been continually exposed to extreme danger. Some of his hostile feelings were targeted toward the circumstances that generated the danger, but most were directed toward the people intent on destroying his plane and its crew. For us, knowing some of the facts without having lived the experience provided only a small, pale, and incomplete picture of what really took place. In such circumstances we accumulate our information in a sterile environment, without the sounds, fury and emotions of war. Out of harm's way and eager to cheer every win, we could not truly relate to a situation where every flying mission might be the last. Each safe return to base was a victory but one tempered by the knowledge that, in the weeks and months ahead, there would be many repetitions of the same dangerous task. Had we been aware of the actual conditions, our concerns would have been a major burden. The combination of Pat's positive letters and the actions of the censors ensured that we remained unaware of the realities taking place.

Although the home base for Pat's squadron was in India, the distance to certain targets was so great it was not possible for the B-29 bombers—or any other plane at that time—to fly that far without refueling. About half of the bombing runs made by the *Mary K* took place in two stages. The plane would first fly from India to an advance base in China, a flight always marked with a point of no return. Problems occurring beyond that point required the flight to continue since there would not be enough fuel to return to home base. At least one day would be spent at the advance base while ground personnel refueled the plane and loaded it with various types of bombs. From there the plane flew to such targets as Anshan, Omurra, Yawata, and Formosa. Raids involving continuous flight from the base in India to targets and return included attacks on Bangkok, Singapore, Rangoon and Kuala Lumpur. Flying time to targets and return, depending on the base from which the actual raids took place, ranged from eight hours to over eighteen. Since attacks by Japanese planes, either fighter aircraft or kamikaze pilots, were always certain to take place en route to targets or on the way back, unrelenting tension filled the long hours of flight.

In returning from certain bombing missions, the planes avoided flying over northern Burma since it was under Japanese control and fighter planes were quick to attack the bombers. However, while returning from a particular mission to bomb Japanese targets, the planes were bucking severe head winds. This made it necessary to take a route directly over northern Burma or risk running short of fuel before reaching the advance base in China. The inevitable attack resulted in Pat's plane being hit and so badly damaged that it had to be brought down in Burma at the closest available field. The crippled bomber landed at an air base that American and British troops had captured on the previous day. But for the Japanese, control of the base remained a sharply contested issue. They remained close enough to continue the fight and infiltrate the defensive positions at night to pour small arms fire at appropriate targets. This led the pilot to assign crew members to guard the plane at night when the Japanese infantry was most likely to move in closer to the aircraft. Being understandably apprehensive and nervous during his tour of guard duty, Pat unconsciously lit a cigarette and the night became filled with the sound of rifles being fired in his direction. Dropping to the runway and wishing for a nonexistent fox hole, he returned fire until the swift arrival of ground troops succeeded in forcing the enemy to retreat. Emergency repairs enabled the plane to take off for India within two days, with Pat forever grateful the Japanese did not shoot with greater accuracy on the night of the fire fight.

Returning to the base in India, even in a damaged plane, was a reason to celebrate. A mission successfully completed without casualties represented the highest kind of achievement. And, while the base was extremely hot and dirty for most of the year, and surrounded by Indians living in incredible poverty, it was still their military home. It was also a place the Japanese attempted to bomb on major American holidays, even though their losses in planes and pilots were always heavy. Occasionally, crews traveled to Calcutta for brief periods of rest and relaxation, a time-out from bombing missions, the harsh confines of the Air Base, and a welcome relief from the demanding routines of the air war against Japan.

For Pat's crew the total number of combat flying hours, from both the advance base in China and the home base in India, amounted to 510. In all, they flew nineteen bombing missions, with five locations being a target more than once. Their assigned plane, number 525, also known as the *Mary K*, carried the crew on sixteen of the missions. On each of the other three missions they used a different plane while maintenance personnel repaired the *Mary K*.

Throughout his time in India, Pat maintained a personal log on the crew's combat activities. To the left of the numbered mis-

```
①  TARGets Bombed By
    GRew 6 (Later Crew 9)
    PLANes Used - 525 - 238 - 354 - 276

 1 - BANGKok    5/6/44  - 10:40
 2 - YAWAtA    20/8/44  - 13:35
 3 - Anshan    26/9/44  - 12:10
 4 - Formosa   14/10/44 - 10:30
 5 - Formosa   16/10/44 - 10:20
 6 - Rangoon   3/11/44  -  8:05
 7 - Omurra   11/11/44  - 14:50
 8 - Mukden    7/12/44  - 13:45
 9 - Hankow   18/12/44  -  7:10
10 - Omurra    6/1/45   - 16:15
11 - Amoy      8/1/45   - 10:00
12 - Amoy      9/1/45   - 10:10
13 - Formosa  17/1/45   - 11:00
14 - Bankok    7/2/45   - 10:15
15 - Georgetown 9/2/45  - 16:10
16 - Singapore 23/2/45  - 17:40
17 - Singapore 2/3/45   - 18:05
18 - KuaLAhumperR 14/3/45 - 16:60
19 - Rangoon  22/3/45   -  8:07
20 - United States of America
                Finis
```

**Bombing Missions
Page from a Wartime Diary**

sions he listed the number of the plane used. From the right of the numbered missions were written the targets, the day, month and year the raid took place and the total flying time from the launch base to target and return. He concluded the first page of the log by listing the twentieth mission as the one taking them back to the United States. They left in April 1945, almost exactly one year from the date they arrived in India. It was a milestone he would remember with much pleasure.

> ② Crew 6
> (Later Crew 9)
>
> Pilot - - - - - - Major O.J. Feely
> Copilot - - - - - 1st Lt. Ray Krahn
> Bombardier - - - - 1st Lt. T.G. Quadlander
> Navigator - - - - 1st Lt. W. Tuohy
> Engineer - - - - 1st Lt. W.F. Tribble
> Radio Operator - - S/Sgt. P.J. Rowland
> C.F.C. Gunner - - T/Sgt. E. Barthol
> Right Gunner - - M/Sgt. M. Olsen
> Left Gunner - - S/Sgt. P. Aboucher
> Tail Gunner - - S/Sgt. C.E. Botter With
> Radar Operator - - T/Sgt. W.F. Matthews
> Of 20TH Air Force
> 793 Bomb Sqd. (formerly 794)
> 468 Bomb Gp.
> — India —
> Battle Stars For
> ① Air Offensive Against Japan
> ② China Offensive
> ③ Palembang, Sumatra
> ④ India-Burma Offensive

Mary K Crew Members
Page from a Wartime Diary

Some might say the crew of the *Mary K* was extremely lucky, and there are probably none from the crew who would dispute that. Perhaps an element of luck applies to anyone who returns safely from the battlefields of a war. Some of what we attribute to good luck, however, is often the skill that comes from a crew operating as a team to increase the odds for the survival of all. Getting the job done under hazardous conditions while depending on each other formed the strongest of bonds, and the awards bestowed upon the crew of the *Mary K* served to recognize the success resulting from close and skillful teamwork. Pat was awarded the Distinguished Flying Cross, the Air Medal plus three oak leaf clusters, and four battle stars. The battle stars were for air offensives against the Japanese in India-Burma, China, Sumatra and Japan. Comparable in lasting importance to these symbols of courage and sacrifice would be the camaraderie that existed among the eleven airmen who flew the *Mary K*. In all respects, they symbolized the many, both in uniform and on the home front, who became known as the most heroic American generation of the century.

CHAPTER **21**

A Long Ride South

◆◆◆

The constant bombing of German military installations, factories, and cities supported the fierce pressure being put on Germany by the allied armies on the West and the Russian armies on the East. It was apparent to many of the German war leaders that they had lost the war, but Hitler chose to fight on. Finally, fearing capture by the Russians and reduced to living in a bunker as the war edged ever closer to Berlin, Hitler committed suicide on April 30, 1945. On May 7, 1945, Germany surrendered unconditionally, ending a European war that had lasted five years, eight months and six days. For much of the world a nightmare of incomprehensible horror had come to an end, as did the mad dream of the Nazi leadership to establish the Third Reich, a German empire that would last a thousand years.

The announcement of the end of the European war sparked massive and spontaneous celebrations throughout the country, and our area was no exception. Church bells tolled, sirens wailed, and horns blew as people gathered to laugh, cry, hug, and dance in the streets. Others went directly to church to offer prayers of gratitude for the conclusion of a war that had disrupted countless lives and filled others with great sorrow and distress. For many the initial joy became muted by thoughts of those who were casualties of the war, the wounded and maimed as well as the dead and those who mourned them. Everything seemed to come to a standstill as the magnitude of what had taken place swept over the land in waves of happiness and relief. It was one of those rare events in life that stays fixed in memory and does not grow dim over time. Our world seemed to pause for a few days as we savored this great triumph, remembered the sacrifices, and regretted the costs. The sense that as united people we had accomplished this together filled the celebrations with extraordinary goodwill. But slowly, reality returned: we had won only half of a world war and the other half was still raging in the Pacific.

My discharge from the Air Corps Enlisted Reserve was effective on May 15, 1945, and it arrived in the mail on May 17. The next day I hurried back to Wilkes-Barre looking for flying opportunities in the Navy or Marine Corps. I found that the situation in those branches of the service was the same as that in the Army Air Force; programs for flying positions remained closed. The Marine Corps recruiter did suggest that, if I enlisted in the Marines, I might have an opportunity to apply for some type of flying position after basic training. That appeared to be a very remote possibility, and I sensed the intent was to encourage me to enlist. Discouraged and not sure how to proceed, I walked around the downtown section of Wilkes-Barre while thinking and rethinking every possible option. Eventually, I entered a small restaurant, sat at the counter, and ate a hamburg while I mentally searched for a solution. With the war in Europe having ended and the Japanese in an increasingly defensive posture, I felt some urgency to take the quickest way into military service, and the Marine Corps offered that.

Within an hour following lunch, I enlisted in the Marine Corps and the process of going from civilian to serviceman moved as quickly as I had hoped. The physical and mental examinations took place the following week at Wilkes-Barre and had all the elements I had read about since intensive mobilization began in late 1941. Standing in line with other recruits, clutching forms and wearing only shorts and shoes, we moved from one examining station to another, answering questions, reading eye charts and being physically examined in every way possible. It was not a place for those who were excessively modest. At the end of the morning each of us got a lunch voucher and a ticket to a movie. The instructions were to have lunch, go to an early movie and return in late afternoon to learn if we had passed the physical and mental examinations. Feeling reasonably confident about the tests, I returned to the lunch counter I'd visited the previous week and ate in a much calmer frame of mind.

My theater ticket was for a popular new movie called *Going My Way*. Featuring Bing Crosby and Barry Fitzgerald as priests, the story line included humor and a very touching sense of reality. Perhaps because of the turmoil I had recently encountered in my efforts to find an alternative to service in the Army Air Force, the tone of the movie struck a responsive chord and made that fine film a memorable experience on a rather important day. Returning to the examination center, we listened carefully as a corporal called the names of all those examined earlier in the day and established two groups. We soon guessed that those in the smaller group did not meet the minimum standards for acceptance, at least not then. Moving the rest of us to another area, an officer told us we qualified for service in the Marine Corps. He gave a brief motivational talk and had us raise our right hand for the swearing-in ceremony. That completed, he advised us that we should be ready to report for active duty at Parris Island, South Carolina, within one month. It was done. I walked to the bus stop to return to Carbondale and thought about the events leading up to this day as the bus made its way through numerous small towns along the route home. Things were not turning out as I had hoped, but it was certain I would soon be joining my peers and the many who had gone before me to serve the country. That thought pleased me.

The war had brought many changes and uncertainty into our lives, but I was slow to realize that many would have taken place anyway, without the war. By itself, the great conflict had changed the face of the nation and propelled us into a future that little resembled our recent past. There would be no turning back. In times of war or peace, however, times change, circumstances change, and so do people. It is a normal development of life, but for me it seemed to come unexpectedly, when I was not quite ready. Pat was married and, as soon as he returned home from Fort Dix, he and Helen planned to begin their life together in a small apartment in Simpson. The continuing close relationship between Ruth and Stanley seemed destined to result in a wedding as soon as his unit returned home from Europe and he received his discharge from the Army. And, after being widowed for about eight years, my mother attracted the serious attention of a man from Whites Crossing, Adam Kustwan, and it seemed quite certain his courtship would eventually lead to marriage.

It was obvious that Adam cared deeply for my mother and wanted to be a part of her life, even though the prospects of marrying a widow with four children made him more than a bit nervous. Of course, the oldest three were all but out of the household and he was very fond of the youngest, Gene. In 1945 Gene was nine years old, a blond, freckled-faced boy with a continual smile on his face. It appeared a marriage for my mother would not only be good for her, but it would also be a great benefit for Gene. Still, I accepted the situation with some reluctance, even though I recognized the positive aspects of the marriage plans and had benefited from Adam's kindness in learning to drive in his 1937 Buick. All the pending changes would take some getting used to, however, and this one was no exception.

While I waited to leave for Parris Island, I began to realize with even greater clarity that dramatic family changes were taking place and more would surely occur before I returned home to stay. I found that unsettling. The rational part of me recognized that the changes were simply a natural evolution in our lives, and at some point I would undergo similar changes. Something within me, however, was reluctant to let go of what our family had become. Together we had fought our own personal war for family survival and won. Not by much, but we won. And in the process we became more than a household of brothers, sisters and a mother; we grew into a family unit whose bonds were forged from adversity and steadily strengthened by an increasing affection as together we overcame each obstacle to our well-being as a family. Too suddenly, it seemed, we were about to go in different directions, and it was not going to be easy leaving home knowing there would be no returning to what we had been. I would need a bit more maturity before I realized that while times, circumstances, and people change, the good things we shared in our childhood and youth remain forever, just like love.

About the middle of June 1945, I received orders directing me to report to Parris Island, South Carolina, the basic training center in the east for Marine recruits. The reporting date, June 26, met the promise made at Wilkes-Barre to have all of us on active duty within thirty days. The notice to report came at a time when the Army, Navy, and Marines were concluding the capture of Okinawa, one of the bloodiest battles of the war. The exceptionally fierce defense of the island by the Japanese came from the fact that Okinawa was literally in the back yard of Japan. Everyone anticipated the invasion of additional islands, possibly those that formed part of the Japanese homeland, and that made the grim pictures and reports from the battle for Okinawa quite sobering. The situation in the Pacific made my mother very downcast about my departure, and she frequently expressed the thought that I should have waited for the draft board to call me into service instead of enlisting. We talked one day of the plan I'd developed in the past to get into a branch of the service even earlier by modifying a birth certificate to make it appear I was a year older than I was. I had read about other young men doing similar things and thought it had some merit. The idea was to use ink remover to take out the last digit of my birth year and replace it with a lower number. But my plan backfired. The last digit smeared to three times normal size and became an unrecognizable blob of ink. My frantic efforts to erase the stain only made it worse. My mother discovered my plan when she found the ruined certificate. After firmly scolding me, we both thought the incident was funny, mostly because the change in the birth certificate turned into a badly botched alteration. Remembering that incident appeared to raise her spirits a bit, but it was clear that, now that I was really leaving, the incident we had laughed about not long ago was not quite so humorous.

My orders had me scheduled to travel from Scranton to Parris Island by train, departing on June 25, 1945. It was a Monday, and the train was due to depart about seven o'clock in the morning. Adam drove my mother and me to the station, and we got there at least a half hour before the train would leave. We stood on the platform near the train I would board, making small talk and watching people, mostly military, come and go. Happy people were greeting incoming passengers while others, more subdued, waited to say goodbye to a departing family member or friend. There was an atmosphere that suggested people living near an emotional edge and the sound and smell of steam locomotives moving in and out of the station added to the mood. Long, protracted farewells are difficult when strong feelings surface, and my mother, trying hard to maintain her calmness and composure, was losing both. For her, the situation was a repeat of what she had gone through before, when Pat entered the Army and later left to go overseas. Now, ironically, he would be home to stay in about five days, an exchange of one worrisome situation for another. It was too much.

As boarding time drew closer, she talked to me as seriously and earnestly as she ever had in the past, intent on giving me in a few minutes all the advice and admonitions she could think of to keep me from harm. Hoping to ease her mind, I tried to be as reassuring and light-hearted as I could. It didn't help that much. Adam stood off to the side, staying in the background, ill at ease, fidgeting, looking pained and not at all sure of the part he should play in this farewell. The conductor's loud invitation to board the train brought the somber little gathering to an end. After a handshake with Adam and a final hug and kiss with my tearful mother, I boarded the passenger car with my hand bag and took a seat at a window to wave goodbye. They moved closer to the coach I was on and stood on the platform looking dejected and forlorn. A whistle signaled departure, and after a few halting movements, the train began to roll slowly away from the station. I kept smiling as hard as I could while I waved, hoping to convey a happiness I did not really feel. I kept it up until she and Adam were out of sight and then settled back for a long ride south.

CHAPTER **22**

An Unexpected Silence
◆◆◆

The first few hours of traveling on the train were quiet and a bit gloomy. Although continually staring out the window, I did not really notice anything; my thoughts were still on the parting at the railroad station. I never anticipated it would be so emotional, and I felt responsible for making my mother sad. Eventually, I began to notice my fellow travelers and guessed that many of the young men sharing my coach were heading for a basic training camp at some military facility. They had the slightly apprehensive look of travelers who knew where they were going, but were not sure what to expect when they got there. I felt a kinship with all of them.

By the time we approached South Carolina, there were at least forty recruits on our coach who were going to the Marine Corps Training Center at Parris Island. We were quick to take some comfort from the large number about to share a common experience; it seemed to confirm our hopes that we were doing the right thing. The conversations were light, sometimes humorous, and often included grim tales about what we should expect once we passed through the main gate at the training center. As the heat increased and soot from the coal-burning locomotive blew in through the opened windows, talking among recruits dropped to a minimum level. We were uncomfortably warm, hungry for a hearty meal, and dusty. The announcement by the conductor that we would get off the train at Florence, South Carolina, to clean up and eat drew a prolonged cheer. The actual stop, however, was nothing to cheer about. We got off in the middle of a train yard to clean up at a single, hand-operated water pump. The food consisted of sandwiches passed out as we boarded the train to continue our journey. I began to think that perhaps boot camp had started earlier than expected.

As we neared our destination, a conductor called for our attention. He was a tall, strong-looking black man, middle aged, who spoke slowly and carefully in a distinctive drawl. He told us in simple terms that recruits could not take any food to Parris Island. As soon as we reached the training center, he said, Marines would take the food from us. He named some of the things we would not be able to keep: cookies, candy bars, cupcakes and fruit of all types. Not wanting to see the food wasted, he suggested it be given to him to share with those in need. His speech was as persuasive as it was startling, and I watched in fascination as he walked down the aisle of the coach, a large bag in hand, and collected a sizable amount of food. This small incident, like the stop at Florence, seemed to make it clear that our new world was going to be a very serious place.

It is unlikely that one could prepare for the chaos that existed for the first three days in boot camp. It was a blur of sweaty, rushing activity accompanied by continual commands delivered at high volume by drill instructors who seemed to be very angry. Among the very first of the initiation rites at Parris Island was the hair-cut. It left all of us with barely a stubble of hair on our heads. With gleaming white scalps contrasting sharply with tanned faces, we looked strange and eerily alike. Following the standard trim, we were constantly in lines picking up clothes, bedding, equipment, getting a variety of shots, and being examined. Drill instructors ensured that the move from one activity to another took the shortest possible time. Any error in following orders, no matter how minor, resulted in an opportunity to get to know a drill instructor in a close, personal way. While a recruit stood rigidly at attention, a drill instructor would be inches from his face, veins popping in face and neck as he loudly corrected the recruit and questioned his mental capacity and ancestry. Although the impromptu educational tirades usually had a specific recruit as the target, it was a learning experience for the entire platoon.

Our barracks was a large, rectangular wooden structure that was two stories high and housed a platoon of about forty recruits on each floor. The floors were wood, as was the white clapboard siding on the outside. Many windows on each side provided the ventilation needed in that hot climate. The sleeping quarters occupied most of the floor space with double bunk beds lining each wall. Bathroom facilities to the rear of the sleeping quarters took up the remainder of the floor space. A line of barracks exactly like ours extended for a long distance along the company street we faced. Between each of the numerous buildings were facilities for washing clothes by hand and lines for drying them.

The first evening at Parris Island we made and remade our bunks until every last fold in sheets, blankets, and pillows was exactly right and the appearance was tight and crisp. The same was true for the footlockers lined up precisely in front of the bunks. The arrangement for each item of clothing within every locker was exactly the same. For at least an hour after I felt we had bunks and lockers in the required order, the shouted commands to repeat the process continued. It was apparent that this was a drill about more than standardized housekeeping and the appearance of the barracks. The additional intent was to have each order followed precisely and instantly. After lights out on that first night, the barracks was strangely quiet, even though most of the platoon was still awake while a few slept restlessly. There were still about twelve weeks to go in this new, intense environment.

Close order drill, combined with training in the manual of arms, was relentless. The fierce heat and humidity of the South Carolina summer made it a very draining exercise. Well before mid-morning, the fatigues became wet with sweat as the repetitions continued endlessly. At times it was a relief to pause and stand rigidly at attention while someone in the platoon learned of an error he had made. The comments shouted by a drill instructor were sometimes quite humorous, and trying to keep from smiling was often difficult. We learned very early in boot camp that being caught smiling while someone was being corrected was a major offense, one that doubled the rage of the drill instructor and shifted it to the smiling target. In one such incident a recruit immediately to the front and right of me was fighting a losing battle to control his mirth. While his lean, wide-eyed, sweating face was struggling to remain composed, his upper body was shaking with barely suppressed laughter. The drill instructor noticed it immediately. Following a lengthy harangue delivered at close range, the now solemn recruit, as directed, handed his rifle to the man next to him. The next command to the recruit was to "fly" around the parade ground as fast as he could run while vigorously flapping his arms and shouting at the top of his voice that he was a "Parris Island S—t Bird." The rest of us stood at attention and, as one, counted the number of times he "flew" around the field. We got the message. We confined our smiles to the barracks area, when drill instructors were not in sight.

Despite the constant demands that we do all tasks better, I was impressed with the fact that we were doing so well so quickly. In many ways it was very satisfying to carry out commands as a unit and hear the sharp crack of rifles striking hands in unison as we executed a manual of arms drill while marching with precision.

The progress was evident. The same was true for the things we had to memorize: serial number, rifle number, Articles of War, Marine Corps history, each part of the M-1 rifle, and some basic combat tactics. Each part seemed to be a building block, and much of what we were learning was studied or practiced in the barracks during the evening hours, especially the cleaning and assembly of our rifles.

There was an obvious tendency by drill instructors to hold the entire platoon responsible for the failures or transgressions of a few. This resulted in intense peer pressure to get those causing problems for all of us to change their behavior or improve their skills. One Sunday afternoon we marched to the Post Exchange after being told we could buy toilet articles such as shaving cream, razor blades, soap, and tooth paste. Receiving no other instructions, some succumbed to the temptation, which was all but overwhelming, to buy sweet things to eat; we were continually hungry. Six members in our platoon decided to buy food since, they rationalized, they had received no order prohibiting its purchase. The drill instructor never said a word on the issue until we stood in ranks before our barracks awaiting dismissal. We knew a major error had occurred when he asked how many had bought anything other than toilet articles. Visibly angry, he had the six who had not followed the limited instructions stand at attention while facing the rest of the platoon. The lecture on precisely carrying out orders was long and furious. It ended with the platoon being directed to remove all bunks and footlockers from the barracks and scrub the entire floor until it looked new. As we carried out his order, the six causing the punishment became the targets for hours of verbal abuse and threats of physical harm, a corrective action that would have made even the toughest drill instructor proud.

Serious applications of peer pressure took place only when some issue affected the entire platoon. At other times platoon members continually helped each other by working together on a multitude of physical and mental skills. There was a sense that we could get through basic training successfully as a group if we supported each other. It was remarkable how the trying experience of boot camp drew us together as a team and kept us focused on a common goal: graduating and earning the right to wear the emblem of the Marine Corps. On one occasion we witnessed an event that strongly motivated each of us to continue doing our very best. As we marched down a main road at the base, a group of about fifteen young men were coming toward us. They were in civilian clothes, carrying hand bags and escorted by a drill instructor. While they had extremely short hair cuts and looked like recruits, they were out of uniform and not quite in step. It was strange. Sudden commands maneuvered our platoon to the side of the road and positioned it to face the approaching group and watch as they passed before us. Prior to their reaching us, the drill instructor quietly told us they were recruits on the way home because the Marine Corps had found them unfit for service. It was a stunning, unexpected explanation, one that seemed to shock the entire platoon. We stared intently at the somber, sad and dejected faces as they passed, embarrassed to be watching. They seemed not to notice us. That chance encounter was one we would remember; it filled us with resolve to leave Parris Island as members of the Corps.

We were getting leaner, faster in executing orders and drills and more confident in what we were doing. Now when the drill instructor entered the barracks and gave the command to "fall out," he got what he always demanded: "I want to see elbows and asses flying through the door at high speed, and when the dust settles on the company street, I want to see statues!" We were also getting used to the long marches and routines and becoming very wary of simple things like volunteering, an action that often led to being selected for an unpleasant duty. We were ready to move out of our barracks temporarily to take up quarters in tents at the rifle range, about five miles from the center of the main base. This was a major event, and we all looked forward to finally firing some weapons.

The six-man, pyramidal-shaped tents stood over a wood floor. Except when it rained, the sides remained rolled up for ventilation This allowed sand to blow through the tent when it was windy and get on everything inside. We slept on canvas cots, and quite often the last thing to do before going to sleep was to shake the sand from that simple bed. Most of the facilities were primitive, and I could visualize the thousands of recruits who had passed through there over the previous four years. We shared one thing in common: the rifle range had not changed very much.

Training at the rifle range was in the tradition of all training at Parris Island: intense, demanding, loud, and uncompromising. Highly organized with attention focused on every possible detail, it was an unwavering extension of the initial recruit training. If anything, it was more demanding in its pursuit of excellence since handling weapons with great accuracy was so essential to success in combat conditions. While we trained to be proficient in firing the Browning automatic rifle and the carbine, the Garand M-1 received the greatest emphasis. This was the standard rifle for both the Marines and Army, the personal offensive weapon of the ground troops.

I'd been at the rifle range for just over a week when my drill instructor informed me early one morning that I had to go to the administrative offices at the main base to resolve a problem with my life insurance. My instructions were to walk the five miles' distance quickly, conduct my business and waste no time on the return trip. I took a few bites of food at breakfast and quickly got started down the road to provide the information needed on the insurance policy. The fast walk and the rising heat soon had my fatigues soaked with sweat before I was halfway to my destination, and I was feeling extremely hungry. At the administrative offices,

I waited for over an hour before it became my turn for an interview. Within ten minutes I provided the information needed to finalize my insurance records and I was out of the building.

By this time my hunger was intense. My skinny frame had already lost twelve pounds since coming to Parris Island, and I was beginning to feel a bit queasy. As I headed toward the road leading to the rifle range, I noticed a Post Exchange was open and began to consider trying to buy something to eat. While I was aware of the risks involved, I was feeling desperate for food. I straightened my fatigues as best I could and mopped the sweat from my face. Then, taking a deep breath, I entered the Post Exchange. Once inside, I moved quickly toward the food section. There were Marines in the store and some civilians but no recruits. The lady at the counter gave me a puzzled look and said, "Are you supposed to be in here?" I hesitated just a moment before I said, "No, M'am, but I am really hungry; I'm walking back to the rifle range." She looked around to see who might be watching and then asked what I wanted. I selected six filled donuts, three with jelly and three with cream, all heavily sprinkled with confectionery sugar. I paid for the donuts, expressed my sincere thanks to the clerk, stuffed the donuts in the large breast pocket on the front of my fatigues, and hurried out the door.

I waited until I moved beyond the main base and reached the mostly deserted road to the rifle range before I began to eat the donuts. Nothing before or since ever tasted quite that good. Occasionally, I would hear the noise of an approaching military vehicle; when that happened, I made certain I swallowed all food and assumed the proper military posture for a recruit. By the time I reached the rifle range, I'd eaten the donuts and buried the bag in the sand. I felt very guilty but not hungry. I immediately reported to the drill instructor, and as I stood at attention before him, he seemed to look at me for a long time. Finally, he asked, "Did you stop anywhere?" I knew immediately that, somehow, he knew I had. Stunned that he had found out so fast and bracing for the worst, I responded, "Yes, Sir. I did, Sir." Surprisingly, he was not nearly as angry as I had expected. He said, "The traces of white sugar around your mouth gave you away, but not lying saved you from some really serious punishment." For one hour each evening of the following week, I had to fill my back-pack with sand, put it on, take my rifle, and march around an area composed of soft, loose sand, a mixture that made striding difficult. It made for a grueling week, but having those delicious donuts when I most needed them made the price I paid acceptable.

Our third week at the rifle range had just begun when we noticed one day an unusual amount of activity taking place among the drill instructors. They gathered in groups for intense, animated conversations, and they seemed to be in high spirits. Though we speculated endlessly about what was going on, we were totally unprepared for the formal announcement the next day. Instead of marching directly to the shooting areas as we normally did early each morning, our platoon and all the others we could see were in formation. The quiet stillness in the ranks was a reflection of the anticipation we were feeling. After a brief wait, we learned that the United States had secretly developed an extraordinary bomb and had successfully dropped one on the Japanese city of Hiroshima a few days before. The real significance of this event was not apparent until it became clear that the single bomb had destroyed the entire city and killed most of its people in a gigantic fire-storm. It was incomprehensible to most of us that a single bomb they called atomic could be that powerful.

The astonishing news caused mixed feelings to sweep through the ranks: elation, confusion, and uncertainty as to what it meant to each of us. We now had the weapon that would ensure victory over our bitter enemy and shorten the war. Before we could dwell on that too long, the announcement switched to what effect the new bomb would have on our training. The short answer was absolutely none. Training would not change in any way because of the expectations that the tenacious Japanese would never surrender. The Marine Corps still anticipated having to invade each island comprising the Japanese homeland and taking each city street by street in hand-to-hand combat. The graphic lecture continued with a harshness guaranteed to keep us fully focused on the basic training that remained. In a short time we were again firing weapons and honing our skills, but at every opportunity we talked about the great bomb.

That night, we explored every possible impact the bomb might have on the war and on each of us. I lay awake for a long time trying to put the matter in some reasonable perspective. I tried to understand first why the Japanese would continue to fight when faced with such a destructive force, one that could destroy their entire country. It did not make sense, and I wondered if the Japanese leaders were being stubborn and tenacious at the expense of the Japanese people. It surprised me to feel strangely sad and not know why. One thing was certain, however: the bomb had altered the nature of this war and all conflicts that might arise in the future. The great bomb had escalated devastation to a new level and was much less discriminate since so many non-combatants were victims of its massive, fiery force. I went to sleep thinking that if there were ever such a thing as "normal" warfare, it had just come to an end.

In a few days we learned that, in an effort to force a Japanese surrender, a second atomic fireball had destroyed another Japanese city, Nagasaki. This time there was a clear sense that the enormous conflict that had raged since December 1941 was all but over. In a matter of days we learned that the Japanese had surrendered on August 15, 1945, and that a formal surrender ceremony would take place early in September, just about the time we would be graduating from basic training. The end had come with an unanticipated abruptness; the war was over and we had won. After years of sound and fury, the world was suddenly filled with an unexpected silence. The victory brought feelings of happiness and relief, but they soon became muted by the fact that I had not had a part in the triumph. I'd been rushing toward a war that eluded me. Our training, however, continued at the same unwavering pace. There was no change in the attitude, drive, or determination of the drill instructors that would indicate the nation had just won a great victory.

Soon, an even sharper reality began to sink in, that the greatest war in the history of man was over and I had missed it by a matter of a few months. Being in a branch of the military before the war ended was not much consolation. While there were some feelings of relief that I had also missed the horror and bloodshed of combat, much greater were the feelings of uneasiness and remorse that so many had done so much during the conflict and I had done so little. I regretted not being a part of that great fraternity of veterans in the nation who shared campaign ribbons, battle stars, and decorations. I thought about the camaraderie that had developed among my platoon members in just twelve short weeks and realized how much greater the level must be among those who shared the dangers of war over a much longer period. My ambivalent feelings included the conviction that there would never be another time like this, a time when the entire country came together in uncommon unity and made enormous sacrifices for the cause of freedom and peace. I had come close to playing a role in this extraordinary historical event, but it ended just as I was ready to take part. My race to join the great conflict had fallen short, and I felt depressed. Then I thought of the great relief and joy my mother must be feeling and smiled at that mental picture.

Graduation was still a very satisfying experience. Having completed the twelve weeks of training and feeling pleased by the sense of accomplishment, I looked forward to finally wearing the

Marine Corps emblem and getting my next assignment. The drill instructors seemed to relax a bit, but we had grown very wary and still treated them cautiously and with much respect. The mood within the platoon was one of a family of brothers celebrating a major milestone in life and getting ready to part company. We compared our new orders when they arrived and the wide dispersal of the platoon surprised us. Most received assignments to other posts on the East and West Coasts for advanced training while a few of us got orders to report to the Marine Corps Headquarters at Quantico, Virginia. We parted promising we'd all get together someday, even though we all knew that would not likely happen.

    I received a ten day furlough before I had to report to Quantico, and on the way home I stopped at Union Station in Washington, D. C. to change trains. It was early in the evening when I arrived and smiling servicemen and women packed the entire building. They seemed to be still celebrating the end of the war and the fact that they were going home. I had never before seen so many happy people in one place. The mood was contagious and exhilarating. USO stands throughout the station served sandwiches, soft drinks and coffee in an atmosphere that was noisy but filled with spontaneous warmth and goodwill. I spent the two hours before my scheduled departure drinking coffee, watching the crowds and talking to veterans of the war. I had come upon this festive gathering by chance and immediately felt drawn into it, even though my uniform was bare of ribbons and rank

    The lines of people waiting to board trains were very long. By the time some of us entered our coach no seats remained. We quickly accepted invitations to stow our bags in the overhead rack and take a seat on the armrests along the aisle. The spirited talk, laughter and party atmosphere had moved aboard the coach. As the train edged out into the darkness and headed north toward Baltimore, Harrisburg, Wilkes-Barre and Scranton, a conductor dimmed the coach lights. That seemed to bring the sound within the coach to a lower level. Then, a small group started to sing, and soon other passengers joined in a medley of popular wartime songs as the train rattled and shook through the night. It was a nice way to be going home.

We remain the children of our time and place. And in the time of my youth in a place called Whites Crossing, that's the way it was.

Epilogue

Our past does not fade away simply because it remains forgotten and unexamined. Putting old photographs and faded documents in dusty attic boxes may push the people they represent to the rear of our consciousness but does not change the fact that they passed this way and mattered. They were ordinary people on a one-way journey making the most of the time in which they lived. They overcame misfortunes, succeeded, failed, loved, lost, and covered the spectrum of human behavior from hero to villain. Just like us. In advancing the quality of their own lives, they raised the standards for we who would follow. Now we take our turn at the head of a long line of ancestors who have contributed to who we are and what we have become. We are as directly connected to those who came before as we are to those who will take the ancestral torch from us and carry it forward. It is a seamless pattern of life that forever joins the past with the present and makes each of us a part of that endless story.

Afterword

Joseph Oblazney

My grandfather never seemed to change very much. His appearance was always one of robust strength. Well into his twilight years, his full head of hair and curled mustache remained blond. His ageless appearance deceived us, for his health was failing and we were unaware. Late in the evening on February 24, 1945, while asleep in bed at the home and farm he treasured, he died as quietly as he had lived. He was almost 73.

Mary Loyack Oblazney

Grandmother Mary lived to celebrate the end of the war and the safe return of her grandchildren who served during the conflict. Her religious intensity never wavered, nor did her interest and concern for her five children and fourteen grandchildren. Her life, however, was never quite the same after her beloved "Josef," her partner for half a century, died. She survived him by six years and passed away in 1951. She was 79.

John Rowland

Grandfather John retired from his job at the Wilson Creek Coal Mine and almost immediately went to work as a railroad crossing guard. He liked being outdoors and especially enjoyed the frequent visits from friends who passed by his post. He survived Grandmother Teresa by seventeen years and never remarried. He was 74 when he died in 1947.

Teresa Layden Rowland

Grandmother Teresa was only 48 when she died in 1930. It is remarkable that the impact she made during her short life would remain so strong for so long. Still surviving are some who knew her personally, recall her unusual beauty of spirit and person, and count it a privilege to have known her.

Patrick Rowland

It always struck me as ironic that a man who loved life and people so much should enjoy both for such a brief time. As a family we were in an early, formative stage, and there was much more for him to give, know, and treasure. Instead, his life and the numerous promises it held for all of us remained unfulfilled when he passed away on the last day of 1936 at age 37.

Mary Oblazney Rowland

My mother married Adam Kustwan in August 1946. They bought an old inn near Honesdale during the same year, moved with my brother, Gene, into the living quarters on the second floor, and operated a successful business for twenty-five years. It always pleased me that the basis of their success was the exceptional reputation established for the quality of the food my mother served at the inn. Though their business life was demanding, she and Adam made a comfortable living and shared a devotion that continued to increase throughout their marriage. My mother died in 1983, about twelve years after selling the business. She was 80 years old.

Adam Kustwan

Following the sale of Adam's Old Elm Inn in 1971, my mother and Adam returned to the place of their roots when they moved into a townhouse located in Simpson and began to enjoy their retirement years. Their happy, peaceful retirement life was meeting all expectations when Adam died suddenly in early 1973.

Patrick Rowland

My brother's electronic training in the Army Air Force provided the basis for a long term career as a professional electrician specializing in robotics and industrial equipment. His favorite avocation for many years, one that reflected his outgoing personality, was playing bass violin for a variety of local bands. He and Helen shared a warm, loving relationship and raised five children in an atmosphere of openness, caring, and fun. Pat still lives in retirement at the home they occupied in Simpson for most of their married life.

Helen Erzin Rowland

Helen's remarkable capacity for caring and giving never changed. While her major focus in life was on Pat and their five children, many others benefited from her unlimited compassion. Her life was a monument to goodness. It was, however, much too brief; she died unexpectedly in 1980 following a minor operation.

Ruth Rowland Markunas

The marriage of Ruth to Stanley Markunas took place in the fall of 1946, not long after my mother remarried and moved to the inn near Honesdale. The circumstances made it possible for Ruth and Stanley to buy our small homestead from my mother. While living happily at this location, they had three children, each receiving the same conscientious care and attention Ruth had given earlier to her younger brother, Gene. Later, Stanley's work would take them to Tunkhannock, a town in the scenic Endless Mountains, about thirty-five miles northwest of Whites Crossing. Ruth still lives in Tunkhannock, a place where her warm, gracious personality attracts many good friends.

Stanley Markunas

Stanley's career following his discharge from the Army was in the shoe manufacturing industry. At Tunkhannock he managed a research and design facility for a nationally known company. He and Ruth were well matched as partners; they had similar instincts for enjoying life to the fullest. Theirs was a marriage of a close and devoted couple, one that ended when Stanley passed away in 1986, shortly before his scheduled retirement.

Donald Rowland

My service in the Marine Corps might have been for a more extended period except for the fact that I met Genevieve Ann Valitsky at a dance in Mayfield while on a week-end leave. We later married, had one son, Don, and enjoyed immensely the years we spent in Annville where I received a degree from Lebanon Valley College. Six years of teaching was followed by a much longer career in telecommunications. For our small family the summer of 1971 was one of sharply contrasting emotions. The joy of our son's graduation from West Point was followed a few months later by Genevieve's death after a long illness. In 1974 Lillian Rosborough and I married and merged families. Living in Carlisle, we enjoy the pleasure of many friends, retirement and our numerous grandchildren.

Eugene Rowland

Gene spent the second half of his youth growing up happily at the inn near Honesdale, the only child in the household with my mother and Adam. On weekends and during the summer months he became a valuable assistant in the business. Shortly after being married to Connie Murowski, he served for a few years in a U.S. Army strategic strike force. Returning to Honesdale, he and Connie raised four fine children while he worked for a major food company. He was a good, pleasant, and very likable brother, and his unexpected death in 1987 at age 51 was a difficult loss.

Mary Lesneski Naumovitz

Following her marriage to Stanley in 1939, Mary and her husband established a home in Mayfield and raised two daughters and a son. The quality of their life together confirmed the sense we had years earlier that this was a couple well suited to each other. Although career demands and relocations diminished our contacts over the years, Mary remained an important part of our family, for she came to share our lives at a time when we most needed each other. She died in 1987 at age 67.

Stanley Naumovitz

Stanley worked as a miner until he was in his mid-fifties. His retirement was hastened by an illness called "black lung," an illness that afflicted most men who worked too long in that industry and inhaled too much coal dust. He lived peacefully with Mary and his children for sixteen years following his retirement. He was 71 when he died in 1983.